RURAL
EVANGELISM

RURAL EVANGELISM

Catching the Vision

KEVIN E. RUFFCORN

Augsburg
MINNEAPOLIS

RURAL EVANGELISM
Catching the Vision

Scripture quotations unless otherwise noted are from the New Revised Standard
Version Bible, copyright © 1989 by the Division of Christian Education of the
National Council of the Churches of Christ in the United States of America.
Used with permission.

Interior design: Karen Buck

Cover design: Ann Elliot Artz

Cover photo: Nancy Anne Dawe

Library of Congress Cataloging-in-Publication Data

Ruffcorn, Kevin E.
  Rural evangelism : catching the vision / Kevin E. Ruffcorn.
     p.   cm.
  Includes bibliographical references.
  ISBN 0-8066-2642-9 (alk. paper) :
  I. Title.
BV638.R84   1994
269'.2'091734—dc20   93-36830
                                                                  CIP

Manufactured in the U.S.A.   AF 9-2642

                                              6   7   8   9   10

Disclaimer

All illustrations involving pastors and congregations in chapters 1 through 6 are fictitious and are meant only to serve as a background or to highlight the point being made. Although reflective of true-life situations, they are not intended to cast judgment upon specific real-life congregations or pastors.

The examples in chapter 7 are taken from real life, although the names of pastors and churches have been changed in the examples.

Contents

1
Square Pegs
and Round Holes

Where there is no
vision, the people perish.
(Prov. 29:18, KJV)

C ars were parked around Immanuel Church late Tuesday night. Lights glowed through the basement windows. Inside, a group of men and women gathered around two folding tables that had been shoved together. They chatted quietly, their conversation punctuated occasionally with laughter. The atmosphere was relaxed and congenial.

After a new round of coffee had been poured and the cookies, brought by one of the members, had been passed around, Pastor Larsen brought the meeting to order. "As you probably know," he began, "we have been asked to focus on evangelism this year. Our denominational leaders have strongly recommended it. In response we have formed an evangelism committee. All of you have agreed to serve on this committee. I want to start by thanking you for agreeing to give your time in this way."

"Well," piped in a voice from across the table, "I didn't know what I was getting myself into, but I said I'd at least give it a try."

Heads around the table nodded in agreement.

"I agreed to be a part of this committee as long as I didn't have to knock on doors and make visits," added another member. Again, heads nodded in agreement.

"I hear a great deal of apprehension in your remarks," Pastor Larsen responded, as he looked around the group. "I think it will be helpful for us to use this first meeting to discover what evangelism is and how we as a committee and congregation can become more active in our evangelistic outreach."

Rural congregations throughout North America have found themselves in a position similar to Immanuel Church.

They have come to the realization that they are called to be evangelists, but they are not sure what evangelism means and what shape it can take in the congregation.

One of the first stumbling blocks rural congregations encounter in their attempt to become more active in evangelical outreach is that they have a false vision of what evangelism is. Both clergy and lay people struggle with preconceived notions.

Rural congregations throughout North America have come to the realization that they are called to be evangelists, but they are not sure what evangelism means and what shape it can take in the congregation.

Within Protestantism in America many people call themselves Evangelicals. They can be found in virtually all denominations. Members of congregations who identify themselves as Evangelical tend to be more vocal than others in their faith and bolder in their invitation to others to enter into a relationship with God. Evangelicals also are perceived to employ a literal interpretation of Scripture, to hold to a "decision theology" (emphasis on making a decision to follow Christ), and to be both personally and politically conservative.

Actually all Christian congregations can be identified as evangelical (in the broad meaning of the term) as they preach and teach the gospel of Jesus Christ and strive to implement it in their lives. "Evangel" simply refers to the gospel. Yet when the term "evangelical" is used, many think of it in a narrower sense and may be reluctant to use it to describe themselves.

When pastors from liturgical and sacramental church backgrounds envision evangelism, they often see it as it has been defined by the Evangelicals. They picture in their minds altar calls and revival meetings, activities that are foreign to them. They struggle with the possibility that if they become active in evangelism, they will be thought of as "Evangelical" and will be forced to compromise their theological beliefs and their church traditions. They shy away from this prospect and turn their attention to other important congregational activities, leaving evangelism to someone else.

Others may have different, yet equally false visions of evangelism. When the term "evangelism" comes up in their conversation, they picture themselves knocking on doors throughout their small town or rural community and asking friends and neighbors about their religious beliefs or encouraging them to become active again in the life of the congregation. Some may remember an occasion when they encountered a vocal Christian who attempted to force a particular belief on them. They remember how uncomfortable they felt and how offensive the other person's words and actions were to them. For some good reason, they hesitate to participate in similar activities. These images are very threatening in rural communities that cherish personal privacy.

Rural communities pride themselves on being helpful and caring. Nevertheless, a fine line divides being helpful and caring from being pushy and demanding. Neighboring farmers band together to harvest another's crop when that farmer is stricken and unable to do the work himself. Fundraising benefits are held to help a family whose house has burned down, or who are faced with astronomical medical bills. A nurse may drop by a neighbor's home and assist in the home health care of a family member. Yet during these times, advice is given sparingly, and personal views and beliefs are shared only when someone asks for them.

These traditions are based on the understanding that in rural communities neighbors were neighbors for generations. This was true as recently as twenty or thirty years ago.

Historically, there has not been a great deal of movement in rural communities. Farms were passed down from parents to children to grandchildren. Small-town businesses were handled in a similar manner. Few people moved into or out of the community. The upheaval in rural communities caused by massive emigration of former residents (and for some towns near cities, the gradual influx of former urban residents looking for a quiet life) is a recent phenomenon.

Unspoken rules and traditions address the issue of the changeless community. The immense challenges of farming and the reality of common disasters such as droughts and storms demanded that the community band together to help each other. The common occurrences of fires, accidents, and deaths gave the people of the community numerous opportunities to be supportive and caring. They understood that what happened to a neighbor today might happen to themselves tomorrow. All of this brought a closeness and neighborliness to the rural community. Yet there were limits to this sense of closeness.

Along with the neighborliness, a strong respect developed for individual privacy. This distance was necessary to balance the closeness. Certain topics became forbidden in polite conversation. A farm family's financial condition was never discussed with them (though it was often speculated upon privately). Family matters and marital relationships were never mentioned. A person might become concerned about what was happening in a neighbor's home, but that concern would never be shared unless the neighbor brought up the subject. Religion was never discussed. The preacher's sermon might be debated, but one's personal faith was beyond the reach of inquiry.

It is easy to see why the pastors and people of rural congregations do not leap at the call to be evangelistic. The very term draws pictures in the minds of its hearers that offend their core convictions and code of ethics. In addition, present-day discussions of evangelism often portray the large suburban congregation as the evangelistic model.

Role models are an important part of learning. We have all had personal role models—parents, teachers, admired adults, or idolized peers. From role models, we learn subjects that are not taught in school, such as what is important in life, how to handle crisis, and how to love. Congregations, too, have role models. From these role models they encounter and learn dynamic worship, effective stewardship, exciting education programs, and now, evangelism techniques. Of course, it is helpful to have role models to which one can aspire. However, this ideal is not often realized in rural congregations. The most visible role models they have in the area of evangelism are congregations that are a great distance from the rural environment.

The most fertile field for evangelism on the American scene for the past forty years has been in suburban locations. These geographic areas are changing and growing. They are seeded with transplanted families and individuals from urban and rural congregations who want to continue to have strong ties to a congregation. Also in these areas are unchurched individuals who are seeking stability in their changing world, some meaning in their hectic lives, and relationships to replace the ones that have been lost due to their many moves and frequent travels.

Congregations in suburban areas usually grow rapidly. They find themselves in a competitive market (both with other congregations and with other activities offered in the culture) and develop techniques to attract new members and stimulate growth in their fellowship.

These congregations are now the models for evangelism thanks to their success and expertise. Because evangelism is a hot topic, these successful congregations are marketing their programs and techniques, sponsoring seminars and workshops around the country. They cover topics like "mass mailing," "neighborhood canvassing," "dynamic worship and evangelism," and "programs that attract." Because of the great differences that divide suburban and rural

America, however, these techniques are not easily adapted to rural congregations.

A pastor of a small rural congregation attended a conference on worship and evangelism. She came away from the conference frustrated and disappointed. In one workshop, the importance of a church choir was stressed. Strong participation in the choir and the presentation of dynamic music were identified as key elements in the congregation's evangelism efforts. This idea was reinforced during the conference's worship times when a hundred-member choir sang moving musical arrangements. "They could give the heavenly host who sang on the first Christmas night a run for their money," the pastor thought to herself as the choir sang a particularly powerful selection. The problem was that the choir of the rural congregation where the pastor served struggled to be a choir bigger than a quartet; on off Sundays it was a trio. Its arrangements needed to be simple because two members of the choir did not read music.

False visions have robbed evangelism of its power and excitement in most rural congregations. The privilege of being a shining light and of sharing the good news of Jesus Christ has been turned into the drudgery of just another obligatory chore. The vision of evangelism in rural congregations must be changed if evangelism is to be woven into the fabric of congregational life.

To change these visions, we must go back to the basics and redefine evangelism. Once this is done, the definition can be related to the life of the congregation. Congregational leaders then can determine what needs to be added, subtracted, and reinforced in order for the individual congregation to be faithful to God's call to be evangelical. A new vision can be created that supplants the previous ones and captures the hearts and imaginations of God's people.

It is standard Sunday-school fare to learn that gospel means "good news." We also learn that evangelism is the proclamation of the good news. All congregations, including the ones in which we find ourselves, are called to be evangelistic, to be proclaimers of the good news. This good news is: "For God so loved the world that he gave his only Son, so that everyone who believes in him may not perish but may have eternal life" (John 3:16).

This proclamation is simple and profound. It is also easily misunderstood. The congregation is at times confused about the word *proclamation*. It has been defined as "judging, forcing, defending, arguing." It means simply "to announce," to tell others that God is a God of love. At other times, the congregation has lost the message of evangelism. People have been told that the congregation needs them—their money or their time—in order to survive. It has been implied that good people belong to a congregation, that the congregation can bandage up their wounded lives, and that membership is "fun." The invitation to be part of God's kingdom and celebrate life that God has given them has been a secondary concern.

Congregations have burdened themselves unnecessarily by trying to measure the results of their evangelistic activities. Rural congregations have looked out upon fields that, although ripe for harvest, are not plentiful, and they have despaired. Memberships that have dwindled despite their efforts have convinced them that they are not, nor can they ever be, effective in evangelism.

Congregations forget that the focus of God's call to the congregation is on the act of proclamation, not on the results of that activity. It is the Holy Spirit who creates saving faith in the individual. Martin Luther put it beautifully in his explanation to the third article of the Apostles' Creed: "I believe that I cannot by my own reason or strength believe in Jesus Christ, or come to him; but the Holy Spirit has called me by the gospel, enlightened me with his gifts, sanctified and kept me in true faith." The congregation cannot use lack of numbers as an excuse not to be active in evangelical outreach, nor as grounds for accusing the members of not being evangelistic.

Congregations forget that the focus of God's call to the congregation is on the act of proclamation, not on the results of that activity.

The typical arenas for the proclamation of the gospel in the congregation are worship, education, fellowship, and various outreach programs. These arenas underline another truth about evangelism—it is both inreach and outreach.

The people of God must be refreshed on a regular basis with the good news. It is the encounter with God's Word that strengthens faith, makes hope secure, and inspires and enables life. It is the proclamation of God's Word and the sharing of God's love that encourage people to return to fellowship and activities with their brothers and sisters in Christ. To say that evangelism means only outreach is to miss a basic, important truth of congregational life.

At the same time, worship is a public activity where people encounter a living God. As such, care should be taken to ensure that the worship service makes the outsider as welcome as the congregational member.

Similar words can be said about fellowship and education. Fellowship activities are opportunities for friends and guests to encounter people who are excited about their faith in an informal social setting, perhaps less threatening than a more formal occasion. Education provides all people with the opportunity to deepen their understanding of God and to examine their religious beliefs and practices. From an evangelical perspective, none of these activities can be focused solely on the members of the congregation.

It goes without saying, yet still needs to be stressed, that evangelism includes both the spoken word and the lived life. It is common to emphasize one or the other. Sometimes people say all the right words, but their actions belie what they say. At other times, people perform inspiring acts of charity and works of love, but are silent and even secretive about their faith. The common response to such evangelistic efforts is that people are left with the uncomfortable sense that they have missed something important, as if they have walked into a movie halfway through the story.

Words and actions must be intentional. Congregations are tempted to believe that evangelism is a serendipitous experience, that it will just happen in the normal course of congregational activities. This idea is expressed by the member who says, "Our doors are always open. If people want to worship, they can come of their own free will. They know they are always welcome here at First Church." One imagines then that a person who has no church background will wake up some Sunday morning with an insatiable desire to attend worship. This person will instinctively know the time of the worship service. Forsaking a lifetime of custom, this person will miraculously appear in a front pew and hang on every word of the sermon.

As pleasant as this thought might be, it is highly improbable that such an event will occur. Therefore, evangelism must be intentional. The worship service is an arena for evangelism, but this does not mean that evangelism naturally takes place there. The congregation is challenged to design its worship service to be an evangelistic tool. Worship must be inviting to the stranger and easily understood by the uninitiated. It needs to bridge barriers, not build them. The worshipers must sense that they are refreshed and renewed to face the challenges of life.

A bazaar, bake sale, or craft sale can be an evangelistic event, but only if a congregation is intentional about it. An unchurched person does not have a mysterious encounter with God when he or she purchases a craft item. To those outside the church, the reputation of selling the best pies in the area is not directly related to being known as the dwelling place of God. A congregation must determine how they can share the gospel with those who attend the bazaar. Doing so might include distributing a brochure that introduces the congregation to all those who attend. A videotape or a picture board might portray congregational activities. A survey might be taken during the bazaar asking people about their needs and those of the community. A bazaar can be more than a money-maker, it can change lives.

In all situations, evangelism must be seen as relational. Stop for a moment and remember how you became an active member of the church. Odds are that other people played a part. It may have been your parents, pastor, friend, or relative, but someone said or did something to encourage you in your life with Christ. In all of the congregational evangelism activities, this truth must not be lost.

**Strangers must not merely
come and worship, but members
must welcome them and make
them feel a part of the fellowship.**

This truth challenges the congregation to back up the advertisement in the newspaper announcing the worship schedule with a personal invitation. It reminds congregations that strangers must not merely come and worship, but members must welcome them and make them feel a part of the fellowship. The relational nature of evangelism underlines the truth that even in this age of mass communication, the field for the gospel is planted one seed at a time.

When we combine all of these aspects of evangelism, we come up with a fuller definition: "Evangelism is the proclamation of the good news, both inwardly and outwardly, by word and action in an intentional and relational manner." This definition says a great deal, but notice what it does not say. It does not say that making altar calls or going door to door to invite people to worship is part of evangelism. Large choirs and a multitude of programs are not necessary.

This definition and others like it can liberate rural congregations to dream dreams and see new visions of what evangelism can be for them. It allows rural congregations to develop evangelistic activities that are tailor-made to their congregational characteristics and talents.

Developing an evangelism program in a rural congregation need not be like trying to fit square pegs into round holes. With prayer and fresh visions, it can be a time of discovery, renewal, and empowerment.

Discussion Questions

1. How do you define the term "evangelism"? (Make your definition as practical as possible.)

2. List several examples of evangelistic activity; also of expectations of being evangelistic.

3. What are your feelings toward these activities and toward these expectations?

4. Jot down some ideas for activities that you think your congregation can develop in order to become more evangelistic.

2
Wounded Healer or Walking Wounded

Therefore it shall be
night to you, without vision, . . .
The sun shall go down upon the
prophets, and the day shall be
black over them. (Mic. 3:6)

A group of people were asked the question, "What is the most important element in a congregational evangelism program?" They had a variety of answers. Some quickly answered, "A dynamic and open worship service," and "diverse congregational programs." One person responded, "A clear understanding of God's call to be evangelical." Another spoke up and said, "Knowledge of the Scriptures." Four or five people, who were sitting together, collectively came back with the answer, "People with a close personal relationship with Jesus Christ." While all of these answers are significant elements in any congregational evangelism program, none of them is *the* most important element. The correct answer is "the pastor."

Many clergy may groan at reading this and be tempted to close this book and hide it in some dark recess of their study bookshelf. Still, doing so will not eliminate the truth that the pastor is overwhelmingly important in any congregational evangelism program. Consider the following situation.

Bethel Church and Zion Church are located ten miles apart on the prairie and have histories that make them almost identical twins. Both congregations were formed by immigrants, and the first church buildings were built within a year of each other. The two churches grew at similar rates as more settlers populated the area and as the local families grew. Many of the traditions they established were similar. Summer church picnics and fall harvest festivals were a part of each congregation's life. Fellowship suppers were scheduled on dates that were jointly set by the two congregations so as to allow extended families and friends to attend both. For several decades in the early years of their history, both churches were even served by the same pastor.

The pastor is overwhelmingly important in any congregational evangelism program.

Both of the congregations have weathered the theological controversies and mergers that have been a part of their denomination's history. The controversies bonded the members of each congregation together rather than splitting them apart. The mergers were endured with the stoic affirmation that whatever happened at the church headquarters did not have much effect on the congregations out on the prairie.

For the past fifteen years, both of the congregations have experienced the economic downturns and demographic changes that have hit rural life in the midwestern United States. Yet, they have reacted to the changes very differently.

The congregation of Bethel Church dealt with changes by ignoring them. Worship services, Sunday school, Bible studies, and fellowship activities essentially remained the same. The members attempted to leave their problems and the challenges they faced at the church door. Problems were not discussed over coffee after the worship service, nor were they given much serious consideration in the sermons or the Bible studies. There was an unspoken agreement among the members that the church would be a place of changeless peace and security amidst the turbulent waters of rural America.

Finally, the dwindling attendance at worship services and Sunday school forced the congregation to look at the possibility of making some changes. They did so with their

focus on survival, not evangelism. The question uppermost
in their minds was, "How can we keep the doors of Bethel
Church open?" Their answers centered on the congregation's
ministry to its members by encouraging increased attendance
at worship and participation in congregational activities.

The pastoral ministry was everything that the congregation wanted. The pastor was theologically solid and
preached interesting sermons. He attended all of the meetings
of the women of the church, worked with the children in
Sunday school, and visited the sick and dying. During times
of crises he counseled with families in a comforting and helpful manner. If asked what the purpose of his pastoral ministry
was, the pastor would quickly reply, "To minister to the needs
of the members of the Bethel congregation through the
preaching of God's Word and the sacraments."

Meanwhile, Zion Church faced the changes that
were occurring around the congregation in a straightforward
and positive manner. A morning prayer breakfast (with emphasis on prayer, not food) was held each week to pray for
the needs of the people and the community. Through a foundation grant, three members of the congregation received
training in peer counseling. This training enabled them to
help the people of the community who were going through
bankruptcies, farm losses, and family strife. A food pantry
and a clothing outlet were set up in the church basement for
families in extreme need. The pastor sought to craft his sermons so that the message of the text addressed the struggles
that the people were experiencing. Local authorities on grief,
stress management, and personal/family relationships were
invited to teach classes on those subjects. The classes were
publicized extensively and open to the entire community.

Several families who were members of Zion Church
sold their farms and moved out of the community. These
departures, combined with the exodus of many young people
from the community, caused the membership of Zion to sag.
However, several families from the community who had come

into contact with Zion through the peer counseling program
or the education programs joined the congregation. The presence of these newcomers encouraged Zion to alter its worship
service so that visitors from other denominational backgrounds would feel more comfortable as they participated in
the service. Although the changes were not extensive, some
grumbling was heard from some of the longtime members
who did not like to tinker with tradition.

The spark for much that happened at Zion Church
was provided by the pastor. It was he who challenged the
congregation to address the issues that confronted them and
their community. He had a vision of what Zion could be and
he shared that vision with the congregation so that it became
their own. When asked what he thought was the purpose of
pastoral ministry, he replied, "It is to minister to the needs
of the congregation and lead them in mission to the world."

Even in congregations as similar as Bethel and Zion,
there are several variables. It can be argued that the combination of these variables is the cause of the congregations'
different reactions to change. But the most obvious and most
significant difference is the pastor. Both pastors are skilled
and capable ministers who seek to touch people with the
gospel of Jesus Christ and make a difference in the lives of
those people. However, they have a very different understanding of what the role of a pastor is and a very different
vision of the mission of the church.

If a congregation is to be evangelistic, it is necessary
for the pastor to carry the vision of evangelism in his or her
ministry and share this vision with the congregation. This
vision is not an intrinsic part of most congregations' understanding of themselves. When people in rural communities
converse about the church, they usually picture in their minds
worship services, Sunday schools, and bazaars. They do not
envision people sharing their faith with others, or supporting
a family in the midst of tragedy, or clothing and feeding the

needy. These pictures will only change as the Holy Spirit moves in the lives of the people through strong pastoral leadership.

Even if a pastor has a strong evangelistic vision of the church, several issues hinder him or her from sharing this vision with a rural congregation. These issues lie buried just below the surface of everyday congregational life. Neither the pastor nor the congregation is likely to deal with these issues unless a disruption in the normal flow of congregational life brings them to the surface. An evangelistic vision of the congregation can cause such a disruption. One of the first issues uncovered is the belief that the pastor is *the* evangelist of the congregation.

Tammy Clark, a recent seminary graduate, was assigned to a small rural congregation in the southeastern United States. She traveled to her new assignment with high hopes and a sense of excitement. As she settled in, arranging her books on the shelves in her office, pictures of what a rural congregation could be raced through her mind. They portrayed a strong sense of the congregation as an evangelistic tool of the Lord.

Tammy knew better than immediately to share her vision of what the congregation could be with the people whom she was called to serve. She had been advised to wait at least one year before making any drastic changes in congregational life, and she did. During that year, Tammy immersed herself in her ministry. She found it exciting and demanding work that drew on all her training and talents. Tammy also found that she usually put in a fifty-five- to sixty-hour week and never had the feeling that she was finished at the end of the day.

One of the things Tammy discovered about the congregation during her first year of ministry was that it had a tendency to be self-centered. The attitude of the people was one that implied that if others wanted to participate in congregational activities, they could; however, no special invitations would be given. The congregation's self-centeredness was not intentional or spiteful. It appeared to stem from tradition and from a lack of vision. No matter what its origin, it disturbed Tammy.

Tammy's congregation, though rural, was located only about thirty miles from a larger city. People were moving out of the city into the surrounding areas to take advantage of the many blessings of rural life. The town was experiencing a slow but steady growth. However, the congregation was not reaching out to any of these people. In Tammy's mind, the congregation was hindering people from experiencing the gospel of Jesus Christ.

At a council meeting, Tammy proposed a solution to the dilemma that she saw. She asked the council to approve the formation of a visitation team. She would train the team in evangelism fundamentals so they could help her visit newcomers to the community. Her proposal was met with stony silence. After a few uncomfortable minutes, the chairman of the council spoke. "Pastor Clark, don't get us wrong. We don't mind having new people come to our church. But we hired you to visit them. We don't think that it is right for you to ask us to do your job for you."

Tammy was devastated. Suddenly she felt very alone in her ministry and confused over what she should do.

Tammy Clark is not an isolated case. It is all too common for congregations to believe that the pastor is the "professional Christian," the person who does all the good works that the other members of the congregation do not want to do or do not have time to do.

Such a congregational attitude separates the pastor from the congregation and places a great deal of stress on the pastor. It gives the pastor one more thing to do in an already crowded schedule. It can lead to "performance expectations" on the part of the congregation. After several months or a year, congregation members may confront the pastor and say, "We're not growing. It doesn't seem that you are doing a very good job of attracting new members to our congregation."

Rather than fighting this battle by lifting up the vision of evangelism before the congregation, many pastors remain silent. They content themselves with a less confrontational status quo ministry that is usually acceptable to the congregation.

Several positive alternatives exist for a pastor in this situation. Education is one of them. Certain basic issues need to be discussed in such a situation. Among these issues are the priesthood of all believers, the role of ordained clergy, the purpose of the congregation, and the congregation as the body of Christ. These issues can be addressed through Bible studies, small group discussions, sermons, and newsletters. Education never brings about overnight change, but it plants the seed for change to occur.

These educational efforts may provide opportunities for members of the congregation to acknowledge and confront their feelings and fears in regard to evangelism. Often the pastor is saddled with the task of evangelism because members do not feel adequate for the task. "I don't know what I would say," congregation members often respond. "What do I do if they ask me a question I can't answer?"

At other times, congregation members may voice some of the false visions of evangelism mentioned in chapter 1. Once exposed, these fears can be handled in a positive and helpful manner rather than avoided.

Negotiation is another option for the pastor. It is not healthy for the pastor to add one more ministerial activity to an already crowded schedule, but schedules can be modified. It may be necessary for the pastor to assume a visible role in some specific evangelism activities. If this is the case, the pastor can meet with the council or with the pastor/parish relations committee, or a similar committee, to determine what can be changed in the pastor's job description to provide time for evangelism activity. Perhaps the pastor does not need to attend all of the committee meetings or all of the Bible study sessions. Congregational members may be more willing to share some aspect of pastoral ministry other than evangelism. Participation in ministry in this manner is at least a step toward joint ministry.

Such activities take time and energy. They are not always easy or comfortable, and they do not produce quick fixes. Yet they are beneficial to the congregation and are necessary in sharing the vision of evangelism. They allow the pastor to become a leader in congregational evangelism and not the sole congregational evangelist.

The low population density of rural areas has shaped congregations and has affected pastoral ministry. Rural congregations are usually not as large as their urban counterparts and members are spread over vast geographic areas.

The issue of the pastor as *the* evangelist is not the only issue that plagues pastors and rural congregations. Another issue that surfaces for pastors is the isolation of rural ministry. Many problems challenge rural America today, but population overcrowding is not one of them.

The low population density of rural areas has shaped congregations and has affected pastoral ministry. Rural congregations are usually not as large as their urban counterparts and members are spread over vast geographic areas. For pastors, this situation often translates into a ministry that is divided between two or three congregations, usually requiring a large amount of traveling. Fellow pastors live a significant distance away. Thus a pastor spends long hours alone and has limited contact with colleagues.

Most of the rural population does not experience the level of isolation that a pastor does. A restaurant or truck stop is usually close by where farmers and ranchers gather to discuss the latest agricultural issues. Clubs and organizations are available that provide necessary social interaction for their members. But a pastor may need to drive fifty to seventy miles to visit a colleague of the same denomination. It may take half a day for a pastor to drive to a meeting for clergy. Traveling to and from a continuing-education event often takes more time and money than the event itself.

This relative isolation is significant because developing a strong evangelistic emphasis in a congregation is a demanding pastoral task. Not only does it take a great deal of time and effort, but it can also be an emotionally draining enterprise. Personal renewal and professional support of the pastor are vitally important if a continuing evangelism program is to be established in a congregation.

Solving the isolation problem is not beyond the means of any pastor in rural ministry. It is necessary to acknowledge the need and act upon it. Attention needs to be given to professional pastoral relationships. A pastor needs to be intentional in the establishment and nourishment of personal support groups. It is important to have a challenging and refreshing continuing-education program as part of one's pastoral ministry. A lack of these important elements in pastoral ministry will cause a developing evangelism emphasis to sputter and die. The pastor simply will not have the emotional or physical energy to see it to completion.

A third issue that is intricately involved in evangelism but one not often discussed in polite church circles is the issue of success. This is not the issue of success for the congregation (which will be discussed in the following chapter), but success in pastoral ministry.

The term "success" is treated like a dirty word in the church. The term is tainted by the world and it is not a biblical concept. Consequently, the church has tended to ignore the idea of success. What defines a successful ministry is never discussed in seminary, nor is it a frequent topic of conversation in clergy groups. Yet, it is a rare pastor who has been able to remain deaf to our society's siren song of success.

Ken Adams was called to a two-congregation parish in eastern North Dakota after he completed his seminary training. Ken had grown up in a large midwestern city and was the son of a factory worker. Except for a short stint as a rebellious teenager, Ken had sought throughout his life to be tops in everything he did. He was one of the key players on his high school football and basketball teams. He was a strong student and a member of the National Honor Society. His parents beamed with pride as he walked across the stage to receive his diploma as number four in his class. They were even more proud when he graduated magna cum laude from a church-affiliated college. In seminary his professors were constantly praising him for his exceptional papers. Ken looked at his life with a sense of pride and a feeling of success.

Then suddenly, Ken found himself the spiritual shepherd for three hundred people on the North Dakota prairie. Within a few weeks, Ken had become absorbed in the demanding task of being a congregational pastor. He led worship services, preached sermons, taught confirmation classes, conducted meetings, fretted over a tight budget, and visited the sick and dying. Ken no longer had grades, proud parents, and encouraging professors to signal to him that he was successful. The only feedback Ken received was an occasional "Good sermon, Pastor," and a rare comment that "Pastor Ken sure works well with the kids." Ken found himself struggling to determine whether he was a successful pastor. He had a nagging suspicion that he was a failure.

American business measures success in growth and productivity. A business person can point to figures that show whether her business is successful or not. If sales are up, unit costs are down, and an expansion is being planned, then success is assured. It is not only big business that uses these measuring sticks for success. They are used in rural communities also. Farmers discuss increased bushels per acre over coffee; they may purchase or rent more land to expand their operation. In these turbulent times, they may take pride that they are able to keep their heads above water for another year and that they are relatively debt free. However, there are no such measuring sticks in congregational ministry.

Several families in Ken's parish lost their farms. They were forced to move to nearby cities to find work. Their departure caused the membership of the parish and average Sunday attendance to go down. Because of lower market prices and higher operating expenses for the farmers, giving to the church had declined. Ken's two congregations struggled to meet their budget. Although Ken constantly reminded himself that he could do nothing about the situation, as a pastor he still felt responsible for it. He felt that he was a failure.

Compounding Ken's sense of failure was his personal financial situation. Except for televangelists, the ministry is not a lucrative enterprise. Ken was burdened with educational debt. His salary was low enough to qualify his children for reduced prices on school lunches. He could not purchase many of the clothes or other items his children pressured him to buy, and he was unable to replace his heavily used automobile. Because of their rural setting, Ken's wife was unable to find a well-paying job to supplement the family income. Ken brought his need for a raise before the joint council when they were setting the budget for the next year. After a brief discussion, Ken was told that the congregations would not give him a raise; the budget needed to be cut, not increased.

All of this took place in a society that measures success by the possession of things. People proclaim their success by driving new automobiles. A luxury model is a sign of even greater success. People are successful if they are able to dress their children in name-brand clothes.

Many will argue that these are false measurements of success. Of course they are, but this argument will fall on deaf ears among Ken Adams and other pastors like him. The expectations of society, family, and personal history are difficult to ignore.

In the midst of his struggles, denominational leaders were encouraging Ken to develop evangelism programs in the congregations of his parish. Ken reacted negatively to their suggestion. He could only see evangelism as another sure failure.

When he thought about evangelism, Ken pictured growing congregations. The congregations that were praised for having strong evangelism programs were all in cities. Much of their growth stemmed from the movement of families from rural areas to urban areas. Most of the time the congregations were large and offered a variety of programs and several different worship settings.

Ken knew he could not compete with them. His parish would never experience the growth that was taking place in urban congregations. His parish did not have the resources to offer new programs, and he did not have the time to design varied worship services. "No," Ken thought to himself. If he couldn't be one of the first over the finish line, he wouldn't enter the race.

Ken's perceived lack of success began to affect other areas of his ministry. His excitement for worship waned. People commented that Ken's sermons were "informed" and "scholarly" (polite congregational doublespeak for boring and useless). Visiting the sick and shut-ins became a chore for Ken. One day as he was reflecting over his ministry in the quiet of his office, he realized that he had lost the joy of ministry. He knew that something needed to change.

At the suggestion of a colleague, Ken's first change was to set a few realistic goals for himself and his congregation. One of these goals was to visit at least three marginal members of the parish each week. Another was to help the congregations' committees set ministry objectives for the coming year. The goals may not have been impressive to many people, but they allowed Ken to gain a sense of accomplishment in his ministry.

Ken approached the denominational office for help in salary negotiations. He knew that his arguments for a salary increase would fall on deaf ears in his congregations and that continued discussion would only serve to alienate those on each side of the issue. A denominational representative met with the joint council and explained the salary guidelines to them. The representative helped them discover some possible solutions to the financial struggles the parish was experiencing. He also explained the denominational salary assistance program to them and suggested they might apply for a modest amount. Through the process, Ken was able to receive a modest salary increase and feel affirmed and supported by his denomination. The intervention by the denominational representative also was instrumental in changing the "win/lose" attitude of the discussion into one where both sides win.

A personal journal was another tool that Ken used to reflect upon his life and ministry. Through his writings, Ken discovered that he had some unrealistic guidelines for success. These guidelines included pleasing everyone, being free of financial pressures so that he could purchase whatever he wanted, and being the pastor of a large congregation. When he was not able to do these things, Ken felt he was a failure. As Ken examined his expectations, he realized they were not only unrealistic, but they were his own creation. They were arbitrary and were opposed to his faith.

Ken composed a more realistic and theologically sound set of success guidelines for himself. He made it easier for himself to succeed and more difficult to fail. Ken's motto for success became, "I am successful because I am loved by my Lord and my family, I am forgiven, and I am empowered by the Holy Spirit for ministry." Ken's formula for failure was equally simple. He knew that he had failed if he did not try and if he did not learn anything from experience.

Slowly Ken's ministry began to change. He regained some of the freshness and excitement that he had when he was first ordained. The sense of failure was lessened and his feeling of accomplishment and success was reinforced.

This changed perspective on ministry and life enabled Ken to address the issue of congregational evangelism. Stripped of the expectation for success or failure, evangelism became an issue of obedience and faithfulness to the call of Christ. It was no longer necessary for Ken to measure himself or his parish by the arbitrary yardstick of other pastors or urban congregations. What was important was that Ken help his congregations discover how they could be faithful to God's call with the talents and resources that were available to them.

Another issue that often presents a stumbling block to evangelism in rural congregations is the issue of pastoral tenure. The congregations of Ken Adams's parish had had five pastors in twelve years. They were not an isolated case. It is the norm rather than the exception for rural congregations to have a regular succession of short-term pastors.

There are several reasons for this situation. It is not uncommon for seminary graduates to be assigned and called to rural congregations. Such assignments are often accompanied by the spoken or unspoken acknowledgment that they are temporary. If the new pastor can last three years without destroying the congregations and without being chewed up by them, it is implied, then a better call will be made available.

New pastors are often uncomfortable in rural sur-
roundings, even though some may have been raised in rural
communities. Their college and seminary education has
opened new worlds to them and distanced them from the
values and opinions found in rural communities. Their theological beliefs and political opinions have often changed. Pastors learn to enjoy many of the things urban communities
offer, such as movies, concerts and plays, professional sports,
convenience stores, and shopping malls. When they and their
families move to rural communities, they experience a culture
shock that is as significant as if they had moved to a foreign
country. This cultural distance between pastors and congregation members hinders ministry and encourages short
pastorates.[1]

Definitions of success also play a significant role in
the short tenure of pastors in rural congregations. For many
pastors "big" and "urban" are two important definitions of
success. Rural congregations become only a rung on the ec-
clesiastical ladder that they believe they must climb on their
way to the top.

These factors along with several others influence pastors to ignore the validity and significance of rural ministry.
The result directly affects rural evangelism. With such short
pastoral tenures, a clear vision of evangelism in the rural
congregation is almost impossible to grasp. One pastor will
lead the congregation in one direction. The pastor who follows
her will lead in a different direction. Continuity, direction,
and persistence—necessary elements in any evangelism program—are often lost in the rural setting.

Several of these issues of rural ministry need to be
addressed by the various denominational offices. Yet, they
cannot be the main source of positive change. Action by national church bodies takes time, and the measures that are
suggested are always shaped by political factors and blunted
by distance. It is wiser for the pastors who are involved in

rural ministry to do what they can to deal with these issues themselves.

All pastors must struggle with the concept that they have not been called by God into rural ministry to sharpen pastoral skills for something bigger and better, or to serve time before their real ministry can begin. Rather, they have been called to minister to people in rural settings who need to hear God's Word. Such ministry can be vital, fulfilling, and challenging. It is a ministry to which God has called them, and it does not automatically have a three-year time limit.

This being the case, pastors can settle in for the long haul and throw out those wardrobe boxes and packing crates from their move. They can share the visions they have been given of rural ministry and evangelism, visions that will take time and effort to develop. They can commit themselves to being there when the visions become reality.

Even with extended pastorates, not all pastors who are involved in rural ministry will retire having served their entire ministry in rural settings. Rural congregations will occasionally receive new pastors. While all hope this will not happen at the depressing rate of the past, congregations will experience changes in pastoral leadership. The challenge is for the pastor to work within the congregation to establish a continuity in the vision of evangelism.

The most effective way this continuing vision can be sustained is by ownership. The vision of evangelism and the congregational responses to that vision must be adopted by the members of the congregation as their own. As long as programs and activities are perceived to be those of the pastor, they will die with the departure of the pastor. Those that the congregation identifies as their own will take on a new life and a new vitality even in the absence of the pastor.

In the book of Micah, God speaks through the prophet and says, "Therefore it shall be night to you, without vision, and darkness to you, without revelation" (3:6). These words were spoken to prophets and leaders who were wicked and who opposed God's will. Therefore, the people of Israel lacked guidance and did not hear God's Word.

The vision of evangelism and the congregational responses to that vision must be adopted by the members of the congregation as their own.

Pastors in rural ministry are not wicked, but they are often wounded. In many situations these wounds have not had a chance to heal. They have been neglected, denied, or constantly reopened. These open and sometimes infected wounds have affected pastoral ministry. They have weakened the ability of pastors to minister and have clouded the visions of ministry and evangelism.

In order for evangelism to occur in rural congregations, pastors need to be healed and healthy. The issues that have been identified in this chapter and others need to be addressed and resolved so that the wounds can heal. Then pastors will no longer be the walking wounded. Instead, they will be, in the words of Henri Nouwen, wounded healers, pastors who can minister effectively to the needs of the people and share the visions of God with them.

Discussion Questions

1. As pastor or lay leader, what are the most stressful areas of your life? (If you are a layperson, what areas of stress in your pastor's life can you identify?)

2. As pastor or lay leader, what steps are you taking to relieve these stressful areas? (If you are a layperson, how do you think your pastor can relieve these areas of stress?)

3. For ordained and lay leaders, how have these areas of stress affected your ministry and specifically your involvement in congregational evangelism?

4. What are some examples of success in ministry?

5. What are some examples of failure in ministry?

6. Given these examples, write your definition of success and of failure. Do they make sense to you?

Note

1. Tex Sample in his book, *U.S. Lifestyles and Mainline Churches* (Louisville: Westminster/John Knox Press, 1990), discusses this phenomen more thoroughly on pp. 69–70.

3
The Fragrance
of Life

For we are the aroma
of Christ to God among those who
are being saved and among those
who are perishing.
(2 Cor. 2:15)

I t was a raw February day. The trees moaned as the wind whipped through their bare branches. People clutched at their coats and hats to keep the wind from claiming them. A near-freezing temperature enabled the low-hanging clouds to drop a mixture of stinging ice pellets and sleet. The light from the weak winter sun could not break through the clouds and was only able to shed a gloom over the landscape.

The weather was not uncommon for late winter in northeastern Wisconsin, but that fact did not make it any more welcome. The people of the small town where I served had endured a long winter. Such weather contributed to their already acute case of "winteritis" and made their spirits as raw as the day. Smiles were few, greetings were curt, and eyes were downcast.

I wanted to endure such a day by building a fire in the fireplace and enjoying it with my wife and family or a good book. Unfortunately, it was Tuesday, the day I had scheduled the distribution of Holy Communion to the shut-in members of the congregation. A packed appointment book would not allow me to postpone this activity, so out I trudged into the blustery cold.

Along with Holy Communion, I struggled to bring the gifts of hope and cheer. The gifts were not well received. The cold and wet weather had caused arthritis to act up in several people. Others had head colds or were coming down with the flu. Most simply wanted to be left alone to wallow in their misery and to dream of warmer climates and healthier bodies.

When I visited Lu in the late afternoon, things changed. Lu greeted me with a warm smile. She walked slowly and leaned heavily on her cane as she ushered me into her living room. The moment I stepped into the living room I caught a whiff of an enticing fragrance. Light and fresh, it was like a soothing balm on my spirit. I glanced around the room to discover its source and I caught sight of a bouquet of roses decorating the coffee table.

Lu, noticing my interest in the roses, said, "Aren't they beautiful? They are from my son. He sent them to me for Valentine's Day." She walked over to the bouquet, bent down, and drew in a deep breath. "I just love the smell of roses," she continued. "I can smell them all around the house, and every time I do I think of my son, his family, and his love."

Our conversation continued and we celebrated Holy Communion together. We did not mention the roses again, but we luxuriated in their fragrance. Their aroma lingered in my spirit the rest of the day. On a cold, raw winter day they reminded me of the beauty and preciousness of life and gave me hope.

In a broken world, the church is to have a similar aroma. God has blessed it with the fragrance of the resurrection, forgiveness, and love. However, many times the trials and tribulations faced by rural congregations have robbed them of this fragrance and have replaced it with the stench of depression and despair. It is an odor that wafts through all areas of congregational life.

Mary Allison bent over the sink and made a full-scale frontal assault on the last of the baked-on grease in a roaster. She was a stout woman who moved with a determination and drive that came from sixty years of hard work with her husband on their farm. Mary was nearing the eighty-year mark and she constantly struggled against a weak heart and arthritis. One would never know it, though, because Mary never complained about her health and she drove herself at a pace that would leave women half her age breathless.

Mary paused a moment from the scrubbing and looked around at the other women in the church kitchen. "What's going to happen," she asked, "when we are all gone? Who will take over our responsibilities? Who will cook and serve the funeral meals and who will work with the congregational potluck dinners?"

Her question met with downcast looks and nodding heads. "I don't know," replied Grace Schmidt, who was putting away silverware. "But it's not just the meals. Who's going to sew the quilts and make the kits to send to world missions?"

"And who's going to work with the altar and hang the banners in the church, to say nothing of planting flowers around the church in the spring and tending them during the summer?" piped in June Kanova as she wiped off tables.

"I don't know what this younger generation is coming to," bemoaned Gertie Meyers as she dried the dishes next to Mary. "When I was young I raised the kids, worked the farm, and still attended the Bible studies and helped at the church. Now the few young women who are still around here complain that they never have time and they would never think of helping us cook a meal for the church. They're too busy carting their kids around to this activity and that."

The conversation continued until the women were finished with their work and went home. It was a conversation that had taken place countless times before. Listening to it, one can sense the deep grief of losing the promise of youth in the congregation and the fear of what the future might hold.

These emotions were not confined to the women. They pervaded the entire congregation. As the congregation gathered for worship they would look at themselves and behold an ever-widening sea of white hair. The giggles of children, their banter and play were absent from congregational activities. When visitors came to the congregation, they experienced a gathering of people who were not very excited about living, but who were scared of dying.

Several hundred miles away and across five state lines stood a small white clapboard church surrounded by Iowa cornfields. The European immigrants who had settled in the area more than one hundred years ago and who had laid the foundation and set the beams of the church had chosen to name their congregation St. Paul's Evangelical Church. They wanted to acknowledge that they celebrated the gospel preached by the apostle Paul, that the just shall live by faith, and that they saw themselves as a mission outpost on the frontier that proclaimed the good news of Jesus Christ. Those immigrant pioneers were a people filled with hope and determination.

Today the grandchildren and great-grandchildren of those pioneers struggle with failure and despair. The hopes and dreams of their forebears have been lost. Excitement over Paul's gospel has waned and its validity in the modern world is questioned. It may be one's imagination, but the steeple bells of St. Paul's that once pealed joyfully to announce the congregation's worship seem to have taken on the overtones of a funeral knell.

One of the situations that has caused a cloud of gloom to hover over St. Paul's has been the foreclosures on several farms in the area. Many families in the congregation have been touched directly by the foreclosures, either being forced off their land and out of farming or by having close relatives who were.

Sid Evans is one of those members. His great-grandparents settled the land in the late 1880s. His family had farmed the land ever since. The home in which he, his wife, and three children lived, though extensively remodeled, was originally built by his grandfather in the early 1900s. When Sid was out in the fields, he not only felt a strong commitment to care for the land, he also sensed that he was very close to the foundation of who he was. He caught himself occasionally talking to the lingering presence of his forefathers, asking

them questions, seeking advice, and sharing the joy of
the land.

The Evans family had known difficult times—
droughts, insects, hail, poor crops, total crop failures. They
had weathered it all. They even managed to keep the farm
through the Great Depression, though they came close to
losing it. They persevered and built it into a thriving enterprise—until the 1980s. Now the farm is gone.

The loss was caused by a combination of things not
fully understood by Sid—or by anyone, for that matter. Sid
walked into the bank one day to get a loan to put in his crop.
He knew the value of his land had dropped precipitately, but
that day he discovered that he had no credit and that the
bank was moving to foreclose on his farm. Sid knew finances
were tight for everyone, but he had counted on the bank to
help him over the hill one more time. The bank's inability to
help Sid left him at the end of his rope. Their move to foreclose
on his farm jerked the rope from his hands.

The auction was the worst day of Sid's life. It was
like watching the corpse of a loved one being sold bit by bit.
After the auction, Sid gathered his family and their few pos-
sessions and moved to the nearby town. He picked up some
work at a small factory. His wife got a job at the truck stop
at the edge of town. Together they began to rebuild their lives.

Sid and his family continue to be members of St.
Paul's, but staying there is difficult for them. Though other
members have suffered the same fate as Sid and his family,
Sid feels that everybody is looking upon him in judgment.
Sid's sense of failure has ruined his self-esteem. His grief has
destroyed the joy and comfort of his religion. His anger
toward himself, other people, the government—and, if the
truth be known, God—has isolated him from his friends and
his Christian family.

The last thing that Sid and others like him are concerned about is evangelism. Wrapped up in their own trou-
bles, they are oblivious to the presence of visitors and the

needs of others. To visit St. Paul's, a congregation filled with Sids, for a worship service is similar to dropping in on a stranger's funeral. A person is not comfortable with the emotions, feels like an outsider, and wants to leave as soon as possible and never come back. The fragrance of Christ and of life that draws people into the experience of God's kingdom is missing.

Black Creek Church gets its name from the small river on whose banks it is built. It is located about thirty miles from a growing midwestern city. Black Creek Church is a rarity among rural congregations: It is in an area that is experiencing a growth in population. As such, it is the envy of many congregations that would love to have the problems of overflowing worship services, a crowded parking lot, and bursting-at-the-seams Sunday school. Yet many members of the congregation of Black Creek do not see themselves in an enviable position.

The congregation of Black Creek feels that it is being overwhelmed and invaded. They see the rapid growth of their area and the changes it brings as a threat to their way of life. The pastor of the congregation has tried to convince the membership that this growth is a wonderful opportunity for them. He has challenged the members to see themselves as missionaries who have the opportunity to invite others to experience the love of God and to participate in the kingdom of God. The members are deaf to his words, however, and refuse to see themselves as missionaries. Instead, they see themselves as defenders of the true faith and attempt to make their congregation into a fortress where true believers and longtime members can take sanctuary from the onslaught.

Carl Dudley and Douglas Walrath in their book, *Developing Your Small Church's Potential*, list several factors that hinder a congregation from reaching out to a rapidly expanding population.

- Local people are committed to the social context of traditional village life; they work, shop, and play locally. Newcomers live regionally rather than locally. They are comfortable working in one locale, living in another, and shopping in a third.
- Local people experience the church as desirably and properly local. Newcomers see the church and congregation as more global in context.
- The changes that pastors often suggest a congregation adopt to reach out to the expanding population reflect the culture of the newcomers. These suggestions place the pastor at odds with the congregation. Members of the congregation see such changes as a challenge to their way of life.
- Newcomers do not seem stable enough to be entrusted with congregational leadership. Longtime congregational members form a voting bloc against the newcomers because of the differences in values that they sense the newcomers hold.
- Newcomers do not want to invest themselves completely in the local congregation or the local culture. The newcomers expect to move on, and their commitments and concerns range over a larger arena than the local town or congregation.[1]

Newcomers are different, and members of congregations that are experiencing growth have a difficult time trusting newcomers because of their differences. Historically, rural congregations and communities have been very homogeneous. The first immigrant settlers in an area often came from one country of origin. Often they came from the same town or geographic area. They had similar likes, dislikes, and beliefs. It was easy for them to establish friendships and to worship and enjoy fellowship together. A stranger was always looked upon with suspicion, especially if he or she came from a different country. The unwritten rules of hospitality would be followed—food and shelter shared and other needs cared for because life on the frontier demanded it—but the stranger would not be allowed to become a part of the fabric of the community.

Growth may not appear to be a stressful situation to those outside the congregation that is dealing with it. Yet growth, and the changes it brings, are as intimidating and as frightening as the changes that are a part of loss and grief. The fear of strangers and of change produces an unpleasant odor that covers up the fragrance of the gospel. People outside the congregation are repelled rather than attracted to it.

These are only a few of the challenges that rural congregations face. Life in rural areas has been difficult during the past several years, and there is little promise that these challenges will ease soon. Although life is difficult, and there are many struggles that are unique to rural communities, life is not hopeless. The hope that is contained in the gospel of Jesus Christ is the hope of the rural communities. This hope must be boldly proclaimed and specifically applied to the rural congregation. Only then will the rural congregation regain the fragrance of life and become evangelistic in its programs and activities.

The hope that is contained in the gospel of Jesus Christ is the hope of the rural communities. This hope must be boldly proclaimed and specifically applied to the rural congregation.

This renewal is not an impossibility, nor is it contrary to the past experiences of the church. In fact, it follows a strong theological tradition. Martin Luther in the early 1500s addressed this theology in his description of "the theology of

the cross" and "the theology of glory." He understood that
the popular beliefs—that affluence and success were signs of
God's presence and blessing, and that suffering and weakness
were signs of God's distance and curse—were contrary to
Scripture. Often in the Scripture, riches are seen as a stumbling block in one's relationship with God. On the other hand,
God is seen as the advocate of the weak, the defeated, and
the needy. Luther proclaimed on the basis of Scripture that
when people see themselves as weak and in need, as opposed
to being strong and independent, they are in the position to
have the greatest encounter with God.

The church has at times forgotten this concept even
though it is addressed from the pulpit on a regular basis.
Rural pastors mutter under their breath, "I sure wish I was
the pastor at First Suburban. I think I could handle their
problems of an eighteen percent growth rate and of donations
being thirty thousand dollars above projections. Ministry
could not help but be enjoyable and rewarding in such a
situation."

In their conversation after a worship service, members of rural congregations will say, "Have you been over to
hear First Suburban's choir? It sends shivers down your spine
to listen to them. I sure wish we could have a choir like that
here. And have you seen their new educational unit?" En-
tranced by the big and the flashy, people of rural congregations easily fall into the temptation of envying the ministry
of other congregations. When they do so, they miss the presence of God in their own midst.

The challenges that confront rural communities today are not new creations of twentieth-century technology.
They have been around in different forms for thousands of
years. Throughout history, when the people of God have
confronted these challenges, they have found comfort and
guidance in the Scriptures. God's Word has given them the
ability to face their challenges, overcome them, and at the

same time share the good news of the kingdom with the people around them.

The story of Abraham and Sarah has many characteristics that are similar to the experience of rural congregations. Abraham and Sarah, too, were people of God who were called out to a distant land. Although faithful to the Lord, they did not have children. They realized, as do the people of rural congregations, that the lack of children threatened their promised dynasty and their claim to the future.

During their childless years Abraham and Sarah learned several lessons about the Lord. They learned that being childless was not a judgment of God upon them. God continued a relationship with them and blessed them in other ways. They discovered that God protected them in times of danger and provided for them in times of need. Their childless years became a time of spiritual growth. Finally, when their childbearing years were supposedly long past, God moved and provided them with a son.

Mary Allison and the other women of her congregation, who had shared their grief that there seemed to be no one to take their place, discovered their similarities with Abraham and Sarah during their Bible studies. With the help of their pastor, they realized that the absence of youth in their congregation and community was not a sign of God's displeasure. It was simply a change that was taking place and a challenge that the congregation was forced to address. The women also came to understand that even if drastic changes took place, such as the eventual closing of their congregation, God would still be in control and God's will would not be hindered. Abraham and Sarah's story comforted the women and gave them the courage to face the future.

Shortly after this, the women served yet another funeral dinner. As they cleaned up after the meal, Grace Schmidt shared with the other women that her daughter Sarah

and her family had joined a mission congregation in the sub-
urb where they lived. A mission congregation, Grace explained, was a new congregation that was developed in a
growing residential area. It had been started there through
the efforts of the national office of the denomination to proclaim the gospel and minister to the spiritual needs of the
people who were moving to the area.

"They are growing like a wildfire," Grace exclaimed.
"The people have been worshiping in an elementary school
gym for a year. Already they have over 180 people attending
their worship service every Sunday. They are going to build
a church building, but do you know how much it costs to
build a church these days?"

Grace paused to give her listeners a chance to make
a wild guess. "Their new church building will cost them over
seven hundred and fifty thousand dollars! I don't know how
they are going to do it, but they are sure going to need a lot
of help."

Their conversation continued. The women discussed
several of the obstacles that a mission congregation faced.
Some of them seemed insurmountable. Then one of the wom-
en asked Grace, "Is there any way that we can help this new
congregation?"

"Oh, I'm sure there is," Grace responded. "Sarah has
mentioned that they need banners to help change the gym
into a place of worship."

"It wouldn't be hard for us to make a couple of banners for this congregation," one of the women responded.

"Yes, and we could take up a special offering to
go toward the construction of the new building," suggested
another.

In a short time the women identified several ways
they could help the mission congregation. They became more
excited with each addition to the list. By the time they pre-
pared to leave, they had scheduled two work days to begin

to make the banners. Before they left, Mary Allison observed, "You know, our congregation may not have any children right now, but I think we have just adopted a child today."

It did not happen overnight, but the fragrance of that rural congregation changed. It no longer had the stench of death. When people came to visit the congregation, they smelled the fragrance of Christ and of life. Two families who visited on a Sunday morning sensed the new excitement and eventually became active members of the congregation.

Sid Evans at St. Paul's Evangelical Church knew that he needed help. His depression was taking its toll on his family. He and his wife were constantly bickering and he was short-tempered and ill-mannered with his children. What really scared him, though, and drove him to seek help was his realization that, when he got in the car one morning, he sat there entertaining the thought of turning on the engine and leaving the garage door closed. After work that day, Sid stopped by the pastor's office to talk.

Sid's pastor referred him to a counselor who specialized in grief counseling. He also asked Sid to meet with him a few times to discuss some theological issues, such as God's power, God's will, success and failure, and confession and forgiveness. Sid was eventually lifted out of the pit of his despair through counseling. He was encouraged to address some of the life and faith issues with which he struggled. The insights he received allowed him to face life with a new and more positive perspective.

Sid knew that he was not the only one who was struggling. Others needed help, yet they were just as reluctant to seek counseling as he had been. Sid came upon the idea of setting up a support group within St. Paul's where members of the congregation and community could come to share their struggles with people in the same predicament.

Twelve people attended the first meeting. Word spread quickly about the support group that St. Paul's was offering. Within a short time another group was formed.

The effect upon the congregation was startling. Within a few months changes were noticeable in the worship service. People smiled, they sang with greater joy, and they talked with each other. The fragrance of the gospel scented their lives. Several people from the community who participated in the support groups decided to attend a worship service. They liked what they saw, heard, and sensed. They began to attend regularly, and after several months, they asked to become members of St. Paul's.

The pastor at Black Creek Church felt as though he had been pounding his head against a wall for over a year. Factions began to form within the congregation, with the older members banding together on one side and the newer members joining forces on the other. Bickering and arguing became commonplace during committee meetings and soon spread to fellowship times. It became evident that the status quo could not continue.

The pastor decided to deal with the problem in a straightforward manner—something not usually done in a congregation. He formed an ad hoc long-range planning committee whose membership included people from the different factions. The committee's first several meetings consisted of Bible study centering on the Jewish/Gentile controversy in the early church. During those studies, the pastor pointed out that conflict was a normal part of church life. It occurred whenever the church faced change. During these conflicts important issues of faith were discussed, at times compromises were reached, and changes were made. When viewed from the perspective of history, it could be seen that God used conflict and controversy to form the church into a more effective channel of the gospel.

The council, women's group, adult Bible study, and several committees heard the same repeated message from the pastor: that conflict could be a creative part of congregational life. Gradually the stalemate was broken. Several forums were held where both sides could view their concerns and ideas. Several plans of action were proposed and compromises were suggested. Little by little, the members of Black Creek began to work together. The changes that were made reflected not only the developing needs of the congregation and the community, but also the strongly held beliefs and concerns of the older members of the congregation.

The conflict and tension are not completely resolved at Black Creek, but they are being used to address constructively the situation in which the congregation finds itself. The members of the congregation are joining hands and reaching out to new members of the community and are seeking to minister to their needs. The spirit of cooperation and compromise has allowed the aroma of life to once again permeate the congregation.

These stories illustrate what must happen in a rural congregation in order for it to become evangelistic, that is, a congregation that reaches out to the community that surrounds it. Of primary importance is the discovery that the gospel is relevant to the situations its members encounter in their daily lives. It not only needs to be seen as relevant but also its message must be understood as something that can be integrated into present-day life. In other words, the gospel must be both preached and practiced. It is not enough to affirm the concept that God holds us in the palm of God's hand. The members of the congregation must experience this truth as they deal with grief, failure, and change.

The preaching and teaching ministries of the pastor and congregation are important channels that proclaim the gospel and help people implement it in their lives. The pastor's role as counselor can also be used to enable this to happen. Even fellowship times can be used to encourage congregational members to struggle with the issues that confront them and discuss with one another how the gospel addresses the issues.

The second step that must occur is for the congregation to look beyond itself. This is not easy to do. For centuries, the church has had a tendency to be shortsighted. Its members often cannot see beyond the stained-glass windows and doors of the sanctuary. The congregation becomes obsessed with its own problems. Institutional survival becomes so important that the areas of mission and service are ignored. This is exactly what has occurred in many rural congregations.

The gospel must be both preached and practiced. It is not enough to affirm the concept that God holds us in the palm of God's hand. The members of the congregation must experience this truth as they deal with grief, failure, and change.

The solution can be envisioned in terms of the classic debate of how to treat a mild cold. One group believes that total bed rest is required (this group includes a significant number of mothers). They prescribe the administration of several cold remedies during the bed rest (this may or may not include huge amounts of chicken soup). This activity forces the individual to place a high priority on the sickness. The good news is that often a cold is short-lived because of this treatment. The bad news is that the person feels absolutely miserable until he or she is completely healed.

The other group, made up of a majority of bosses and the "inner voices" of many employees, asserts that taking two aspirin and then getting involved in work is a better treatment. They point out that when one becomes absorbed in work or other activities, one forgets about the cold. Getting over a cold this way may take a little longer, but a person can still accomplish a great deal even when feeling mildly ill.

Certainly the situations and challenges that confront a rural congregation cannot be ignored, but they should never supersede the ministry of the congregation. The members of the congregation might also discover that their problems appear less significant when they involve themselves in ministry.

Once the congregation looks away from itself, it needs to recognize the needs of the people and communities that surround it. More than just a quick glance will be needed because individual and community needs are often well hidden. In many cases, they are ignored and denied.

One of the most commonly denied needs of people in a rural community is their need to hear the gospel and become participants in God's kingdom. Congregational members wrongly believe that a vast majority of the people in their community belong to a congregation. Comforted by this false belief, they do not feel the necessity to be purposeful in their evangelical outreach. "After all," they ask, "why should we try to fix something that isn't broken?"

If congregations do not see the missionary field at their door, they may die—and should.

In reality over forty percent of the people in an average rural community can be classified as unchurched. (Yes, this is even true in the Midwest and the Bible belt.) These include people who have never been members of a congregation and those who have not participated in a church service for five years or more. When these people are counted along with the marginal members who are a part of every congregation, the mission field that lies before the average rural congregation is vast.

Each congregation must realize that it is not a Christian church in a Christian country, but a mission outpost in a vast mission field. Bishop Herbert Chilstrom of the Evangelical Lutheran Church in America stated, "If congregations do not see the missionary field at their door, they may die—and should."[2]

To proclaim the gospel, to invite people to participate in the kingdom of God, and to minister to the physical as well as spiritual needs of people has been the mission of the church since the day of Pentecost. This mission has not changed even when the church has been confronted with significant challenges and obstacles. Every congregation, rural as well as suburban and urban, is a part of this continuing mission. It is the gospel and this mission to which the congregation calls Christians that give it the fragrance of Christ and of life, enabling the congregation to be the hands of God reaching out to a needy world.

Discussion Questions

1. What are the changes that are taking place in your community?

2. What are the emotions that community members experience when they deal with these changes?

3. How does the gospel address these issues?

4. Make a list of ways you think your congregation could address these issues and minister to these needs.

Notes

1. Carl Dudley and Douglas Walrath, *Developing Your Small Church's Potential* (Valley Forge, Pa.: Judson Press, 1988), 22–27.

2. Bishop Herbert W. Chilstrom in his remarks to the 1991 Churchwide Assembly of the Evangelical Lutheran Church in America as reported by *The Lutheran*, Oct. 23, 1991, p. 31.

4
Shaking
the Pillars

So if anyone is
in Christ, there is a new creation:
everything old has passed away;
see, everything has become new!
(2 Cor. 5:17)

I t is inevitable: Evangelism brings change. Evangelism is not the only source of change. Life in Christ, both individual and corporate, causes change. Christians officially expect change in individual lives and question the validity of one's encounter with Christ if change does not occur. At the same time, Christians secretly dread change in their congregation and church and tend to view all change as satanically inspired—if not satanic, at least proposed by a pastor who is confused and does not understand the entire situation.

**Evangelism brings change.
Evangelism is not the only source
of change. Life in Christ,
both individual and corporate,
causes change.**

Sharon Smith-Larsen practices her ministry in rural Kansas. Her congregation consists mostly of wheat farmers and their families. About one hundred of them attend Sunday worship services at the white clapboard church standing in the middle of the wheat fields at the junction of two county roads. The Sunday worship attendance represents less than one-third of the people who are still officially on the rolls of the congregation.

Sharon had been serving faithfully and gaining the trust of the congregation for more than two years. During that time, she had become interested in the subject of evangelism. She read several books on the topic and discovered in them a common theme. The theme was simple: If a congregation was going to be evangelistic, it was necessary for the members of the congregation to see themselves as evangelists.

The people of her congregation were very quiet about their faith. It was unusual for them to discuss faith outside of church. They relied on the pastor to be the congregation's official spokesperson and evangelist. If a new family moved near them, they would mention it to Sharon after services on Sunday and expect her to follow up with a visit. If a theological controversy arose, they would ask Sharon to intervene. One member came up to Sharon and said, "My daughter's home from college and she's picked up some odd ideas. I'd sure appreciate it if you'd stop by the house someday and straighten her out."

Sharon thought that education would be the solution to this problem. These people did not talk about their faith because they did not know how to and therefore the subject made them feel uncomfortable, she reasoned. Sharon determined that she would teach a class on sharing one's faith.

She approached the council with her idea. The meeting was running late that night, so no one wanted to talk about it. They received the idea in silence and just looked down at the table in front of them. After a few moments, the council president turned to Sharon and said, "I see nothing wrong with your teaching a class like this, Pastor. If you want to do it, go ahead."

Armed with the approval of the council, Sharon cleared six Tuesday evenings in her schedule and began to announce the class at Sunday worship and talk about it privately to a few people. Sharon was surprised that little interest was expressed in the class. Still, she obtained a few provisional promises to attend and thought she had enough people to start the class.

Sharon was devastated when no one showed up for the first class. She felt betrayed. The weather was not a factor. There was nothing going on at the high school; she had

checked that out before. When she called the people who had
given her a provisional "yes," they explained that they did
not feel very well and thought they might be coming down
with something—classic symptoms of the apathy flu.

At the next council meeting Sharon vented her dis-
appointment. When she was finished, a silence hung over
the room. The silence was finally broken when one of the
members said, "But Pastor, I don't see what you're so angry
about. People don't want to learn about evangelism because
it's not their job. That's what we hired you for."

Another council member chimed in, "It's nothing
against you, Pastor, don't get us wrong. But, who are we
going to talk to? I'm related to just about everyone in this
community and so is every member of this council. I know
I don't want to stir up anything in my family. You can talk
to them about God, but I know that I can't!"

As Sharon looked around the room, she saw heads
nodding in agreement. She knew that these two men spoke
for the council and the congregation.

Sharon pondered the reaction of the council in the
days that followed. She realized that she had made significant
mistakes in the manner in which she introduced her idea for
change. She had not given enough time and opportunities
for the members of the congregation to voice their opinions
and concerns. This failure to provide for responses led to a
second mistake: Sharon had underestimated the amount of
change perceived by the congregation. What seemed a simple
step for her was a gigantic leap for her congregation.

About one hundred miles down the road from Sharon, Bob Krider, pastor of First Church, was struggling to
introduce some changes in his congregation. First Church was
located in a small town of thirteen hundred, one block off
Main Street and two blocks from the intersection that local
residents referred to as "downtown." The church building
had been constructed in the early 1900s. It had been renovated

in 1950; no more than necessary upkeep had been performed on the building since that time.

Bob believed that the congregation needed to build an addition to the church structure. It was not that the congregation was growing out of their building; worship attendance had been rather stable over the last couple of years, but the church lacked an adequate entryway and rest rooms. The present entryway allowed only room for the people to hang their coats and to process in and out of the sanctuary. The limited space did not encourage people to visit with each other before or after the services and to experience the joy of Christian fellowship.

The church did have rest rooms, but they were located in the basement underneath stairways on either side of the kitchen. One stairway led up to the sacristy, the other to an anteroom beside the chancel. Anyone who needed to use these facilities felt like a rat in a maze. People were forced to descend steep steps, negotiate a constantly changing path through tables and chairs, avoid tripping over the sump pump and floor drains, and finally locate a light switch that was several feet from the door among a cluster of switches. All this had to be done without directional signs and in the gloom of a basement lit only by the faint glow of the exit signs. For a longtime member of First Church, a trip to the rest room was more of an adventure than an inconvenience, although occasionally even a member would emerge from the basement with a stubbed toe or bruised hip. For the visitor to the church, however, the expedition was an almost insurmountable challenge.

Bob was concerned that the entryway and rest rooms were affecting the vitality of the congregation. Sunday morning was one of the few times that the members of the congregation saw one another. They, like their urban counterparts, were affected by the hectic pace of society. People no longer stopped by neighbors' homes on Sunday afternoons or quiet summer evenings to visit and enjoy one another's company.

Conversations were limited to chance encounters like those on Sunday morning. But no one wanted to say more than a few words or offer a brief greeting while being bumped and jostled in the crowded entryway.

If anyone was mildly interested in becoming a member of First, Bob thought that the rest rooms would chase them away. Any time a visitor sought the rest room, he or she was "told" in a silent yet effective way that he or she was an outsider and really did not belong. Parents who used the rest room to change an infant's diaper were frustrated at the close quarters and the lack of a counter on which to lay the child. In a society that places so much importance on service and convenience, people would not tolerate such conditions. They would go to another church that had adequate facilities.

Bob tried to share his concerns and ideas with the congregational members, but he met with firm resistance. "Pastor," one member said, "we can't take on a project like this. Times are hard on our farms and in our businesses. We just don't have the money."

Another member commented, "I don't see why we have to spend money on building a new entryway. That entryway has served us well all these years and no one has complained about it. If people want to visit, let them go down to the basement and visit. There is plenty of room down there."

One of the women raised her voice in protest over the idea of new rest rooms. "We don't need those," she said. "I raised seven children in this church. I did just fine with them without some fancy diaper station. Those young mothers can do the same."

The intensity of the comments made it clear to Bob that the members of the congregation perceived more and greater changes than an addition to the building. These perceived changes would need to be addressed if the addition was to be built.

Evangelism spurs change and change is accompanied by conflict. The conflict is not proportional to the degree of change perceived by the pastor; it is, rather, proportional to the degree of change perceived by the congregation.

A majority of congregations fears conflict and avoids it at all costs. Any changes are thwarted because of the conflict they bring. This fear paralyzes congregations in their attempts to become evangelistic. If a congregation is to become evangelistic, it must face its fear. This is best done by understanding the process of change and learning the rules for managing conflict.

Motivation and preparation are the factors in the first step in the process of change. It is at this point that the foundation for the change is laid.

Harvey Seifert and Howard Clinebell, Jr., have proposed a five-step cyclical process of change. This process consists of (1) motivation and preparation, (2) diagnosis of the problem and consideration of alternative courses of action, (3) the formulation of a strategy, (4) carrying out the plan of action, and (5) review, evaluation, and the stabilization of change.[1] Viewing the changes that occur in a congregation from the perspective of Seifert and Clinebell's process, we are able to catch a glimpse of the obstacles that we often stumble over.

Motivation and preparation are the factors in the first step in the process of change. It is at this point that the foundation for the change is laid. In the congregation this step is often ignored or neglected, and the results are disastrous. Change is attempted, but lacking the support that proper motivation inspires, it is opposed by various members.

They are able to marshal enough effort either to hamper the change or to prevent it from taking place. After any unsuccessful effort to change, further attempts to regroup and reinstate change are stifled by protests that "we tried that and it didn't work."

Sharon Smith-Larsen realized, upon reflection, that the members of her congregation did not share her level of motivation in regard to a class on witnessing. She saw marginal members of the congregation being unintentionally excluded from conversations, and people of the community within earshot of the church not hearing the gospel. She was motivated to initiate change because she saw something within the congregation that was not right and that could be changed.

The members of Sharon's congregation did not share her perspective, however. For as long as they could remember, the pastor had always been the congregational evangelist. In the past, pastors had accepted this role without a murmur. The members felt that the pastor's theological training enabled the pastor to accomplish feats beyond the abilities of the laity, and their discomfort with the Scripture prevented them from expressing their faith except in the safe confines of the church.

During the Sunday morning adult forums, Sharon begin to motivate the members of the congregation. One morning she asked members to share how they became active in the congregation. They talked about the effects parents and family, teachers, friends, neighbors, and coworkers had on their lives. Sharon helped them to see that without exception they were active in the congregation because another person had encouraged them. In another forum, the group discussed the roles of clergy and laity and dealt with expectations and misconceptions. Other issues, such as society's pluralism, personal fears of rejection, and lack of scriptural knowledge, were addressed in later forums. Through these forums the members of the congregation slowly recognized a discrepancy between their call as followers of Christ and their present situation. This perceived discrepancy motivated them toward change and laid the groundwork for Sharon to offer her class on witnessing.

It was clear to Bob Krider that the congregation of First Church was not motivated to change. They did not see the need. The status quo was good enough for them. If changes were to take place, it would be necessary for the needs to be clearly apparent to members of the congregation.

The seeds for change were planted in an odd way at First Church. While waiting for the church council to begin, a council member shared his experience of worshiping at a Florida congregation while vacationing there with his wife. He commented that after the worship service the congregation served refreshments in the church entryway. During this fellowship time, several members of the congregation took the opportunity to talk with the visitors. "They made us feel so welcome and comfortable," he said.

In response to these comments, three other members of the council shared their recollections of fellowship opportunities in other congregations. They, too, could recall how enjoyable it had been and how welcome they had felt.

Bob seized the opportunity to capitalize on these comments. He guided the discussion into an exploration of the possibility of something similar at First Church. "Do you think something like that would work here?" he asked. "Would you have stayed to visit if the fellowship area was down in the basement rather than the entryway?" he quizzed. Their responses started the wheels turning for change at First Church.

Further motivation came from a member's grandchild. A daughter of congregation members lived on the West Coast. She returned that fall with her husband and newborn son to visit her parents. The family worshiped together on Sunday. During the service, the baby's diaper needed to be changed. The daughter and grandmother's experience in the cramped quarters of the women's rest room convinced them that something needed to be changed besides the child's diaper.

The grandmother wasted no time in expressing her disgust with the situation at her circle Bible study and at the general meeting of the women of the congregation. Another woman from the congregation, hearing the grandmother's comments, recalled the remarks her daughter had made after she had been forced to use the rest room to change her child. What had been adequate for sons and daughters was clearly not suitable for grandchildren. Thus motivated, the women of the church began to push for change.

Once motivated, the second step is to diagnose the problem and explore alternative courses of action. At this point, congregations often become bogged down and lose the initiative created by the motivation.

The second step is to diagnose the problem and explore alternative courses of action.

Endless hours are consumed by councils, committees, and conversations pondering a problem that a congregation faces. It is examined from every conceivable angle. References are made to similar problems encountered by congregations from all parts of the country. Detailed histories of the problem are developed and shared, but little time is devoted to examining alternate courses of action.

Once a problem and its source is identified, attention should be focused on possible solutions. Various groups within the congregation can hold brainstorming sessions. Their ideas can then be funneled to those individuals who are empowered to formulate a plan of action. Not only does this process build upon the momentum that develops from proper motivation, it also lifts the mood of despair in the congregation caused by fixating on a problem and replaces it with the hope of possibilities.

The ideas birthed through the brainstorming process are culled until a specific strategy is identified and adopted (step 3). Next comes the plan of action (step 4). It is at the point of initiating this plan that the next major stumbling block is encountered: impatience. Both pastors and congregational members want immediate results from any change that is implemented. But this desire is unrealistic. It takes time for changes to have their full effect. Many people forget this and abandon the change before they have allowed enough time to bring about the desired results.

Sharon Smith-Larsen was eventually able to gather enough members for her witnessing class. A total of eight people attended all ten sessions, and all of them felt that the class was beneficial and well worth their time. Even so, they did not rush off and openly share their faith with everyone they met. Sharon's congregation did not see any immediate changes stemming from this witnessing class. The changes came slowly.

The first noticeable change was in the congregation itself. The eight members who had taken the class had become interested in evangelism. When discussing various issues that confronted the congregation, these members would make their comments with an evangelistic concern. They also began to share with other members of the congregation their joy in being a participant in the witnessing class. Several members approached Sharon with the request that she teach another class.

Over time, people from outside the congregation visited its worship services or other activities. A comment made by one of the original eight over a cup of coffee had sparked the interest of a neighbor. The listening ear of another class member had been helpful to a coworker. All were the results of the small changes made by the witnessing class.

Not many people stayed for the first fellowship hour in the new entryway of First Church. They were not used to lingering after the service and only stayed long enough to have a cup of coffee before heading to their cars. Bob had a few doubts at first. He wondered if he had made a mistake in leading the congregation toward remodeling. But slowly the change began to have its effect. Members began to stay longer. Some pulled up chairs and sat in circles to share the events of the preceding week and renew friendships. Several months after the entryway was dedicated, it was fulfilling its purpose beyond Bob's dreams and the expectations of many members.

After adequate time has passed, it is necessary to review the changes and evaluate their results (step 5). In this imperfect world, congregations rarely get everything right the first time—even with the guidance of the Holy Spirit. Anything from slight alterations to major changes in the strategy may need to be made in order to achieve the desired goals. These alterations should not be seen as a confession of weakness or failure. Rather, they can be seen as signs of health and life. The people of God are moving and reaching out to others with the good news. The Greek philosopher who stated that the only constant is change (one might add, even in the church) is constantly being proven correct!

Several other important pieces of information are helpful as one considers the changes needed to encourage evangelism in the congregation. This book will only touch

lightly upon them. A more complete discussion of these con-
cepts is found in Lyle Schaller's book, *The Change Agent*.[2]

One of the most helpful ideas for a rural pastor in
initiating change is to begin with a small group. There are
many advantages to this tactic.

- Organizing change is easier in a small group than in
  a large one. It does not demand as much time or
  effort and it is not as complicated.
- Change is usually not perceived to be as great a risk
  in a small group. The effects of failure are not perceived to be as large. Therefore, a small group is
  more open to the possibility of change.
- Once a small group accomplishes a successful
  change, it is easy to spread the change to the larger
  group.

Sharon Smith-Larsen used the Sunday morning
adult forum as a small group in which to accomplish her
change. She helped the people in that group to see the need
for change and obtained their support for the class on witnessing. Sharon then used the people in her witnessing class
as another small group for change. They shared with others
in the congregation the benefits they had received from the
class. By doing this, the members of the class created a desire
in the congregation's membership for further change.

As the pastor leads the congregation in change, it is
helpful for him or her to be seen as an innovator. An innovator
is not an opponent of the old; rather an innovator is a proponent of the new.[3] This factor is important for all pastors to
understand, but it is especially important for the young, first-
or second-call pastor.

Rural congregations often experience pastorates of
short duration. Each pastor has his or her own ideas, habits,

and ways of doing things. All too often, because of a complex web of insecurity and authority issues, the new pastor feels the need to dismantle the work of the previous pastor(s) and build the congregation in his or her own image. What the congregation was once told was good by the previous pastor is now identified as bad by the new pastor.

Congregations quickly tire of constant change being thrust upon them. They see it, quite rightly, as change for the sake of change and begin to oppose it. It is not long before any suggestion of change by the pastor is ignored. This situation is unfortunate because the congregation then begins to stagnate and becomes blind to valid potential areas of growth and change.

Bob Krider inadvertently stumbled into this error when he tried to institute the remodeling in First Church. He disliked the old rest rooms and crowded entryway so much that he constantly made reference to how bad they were. His conversation began to focus on the negative of the old rather than the positive of the new.

The members of the congregation were insulted by Bob's approach. What had been good enough for other pastors was suddenly not good enough for this pastor. They dug in their heels against change. It was not until Bob began to stress the positive aspects of new rest rooms and a larger entryway and allow the negative aspects of the old to be self-evident that movement toward change could be made.

As Bob discovered, all the parties involved have a much more positive experience if the pastor makes every effort to be seen as a proponent of the new rather than an enemy of the old. Dwelling on the old saps strength from the congregation, while a clear vision of the future and the possibilities that it holds draws people into activities that will eventually make that vision a reality.

The innovative pastor, as a proponent of the new, will always take time to work through the established structure of the congregation. Attempted end runs by the pastor never succeed in a congregation. The established structure of the congregation usually includes the annual meeting, the church council, and the women's group; informally, it may even include the group that meets for coffee each morning at the local bakery. This structure has not only been set up to guide the activities of the congregation, it also allows people to express their support or opposition to proposed changes.

All the parties involved have a much more positive experience if the pastor makes every effort to be seen as a proponent of the new rather than an enemy of the old.

There are times when the process seems to stifle change. Ideas get bogged down in committees. Individuals fail to obtain the needed information in time for scheduled discussion. Less important issues always seem to distract the leadership. Pastors tend to respond to these situations with impatience; they are tempted to take their ideas for change and run with them. To do so almost always spells disaster for the proposed change.

Members of the congregation must be given the opportunity to express their opposition to any change. If they do not have this opportunity, they will work against the change when attempts are being made to implement it. Once they have been able to express their opposition, they may come to support the change if they discover they are in the minority.

Open communication is beyond a doubt the most important tool in the motivation, implementation, and stabilization of change. Unfortunately, it is among the first casualties in congregational conflict. Tempers flair, hurtful words are spoken, and in a few moments communication is destroyed. Often the wounds that are inflicted are ignored in the hope that they will be healed by time. Light scratches may heal with the passage of time, but anything more serious has the tendency to become infected with anger and hate. Like all infections, if such a wound is not treated promptly and properly it will make the entire body ill.

Open and free communication should be the goal of every congregational discussion. In order for this to happen, dissent must be depersonalized. The point must be stressed that those who disagree with us are not our enemies. They are our brothers and sisters in Christ. The opposition has been baptized in the same font, communed at the same table, lived in a relationship with the same God, and are led and empowered by the same Holy Spirit. The congregation comes together as the people of God to face the challenges and implement changes. Unanimity may not be attained, but consensus can be reached.

Change in a congregation takes time. Fortunately, most of the situations that face rural congregations do not require immediate responses. The time used to lay a good foundation for change is time well spent. It ensures that the changes made will have the best possibility of succeeding.

Changes need to be made in order for a congregation to become more active in evangelistic outreach. Further changes will occur when the congregation becomes more evangelistic. While the nature of these changes is constantly fluctuating, the process of change does have specific characteristics that are helpful to understand and use. Knowledge of these characteristics will not ensure the absence of conflict, but it will enable those involved to make the conflict a positive one and to inspire growth within the congregation. The positive by-products of change open the door for a bolder proclamation of the gospel and a more effective ministry to the needs of the people.

Discussion Questions

1. What changes need to be made to allow your congregation to be more evangelistic?

2. Prioritize the list that you made in response to the previous question.

3. What resources do you and your congregation have to bring about these changes?

4. What resistance to these changes will you encounter?

Notes

1. Harvey Seifert and Howard J. Clinebell, Jr., *Personal Growth and Social Change* (Philadelphia: Westminster Press, 1969), 83–93.

2. Lyle E. Schaller, *The Change Agent* (Nashville: Abingdon Press, 1972).

3. Ibid., 55.

5
Back to
the Basics

So faith comes from
what is heard, and what is heard
comes through the word of Christ.
(Rom. 10:17)

High Plains Church faces several challenges. In this aspect, it is similar to hundreds of congregations in rural America. It is located in an area that is slowly changing. The fields surrounding it were once dotted with small family farms. The families were large and children were everywhere. It was not uncommon for grandparents, parents, and several siblings to live just down the road from one another. This clustering of extended families is no longer common.

People are leaving the area. As young people grow up and graduate from high school, they leave the community and do not return. Some young farm families are selling out because they are not able to make a living in agriculture. The main ones who are staying are the older people who sometimes feel as though they are shackled to their farms. This population movement has caused the median age of the area to rise, so much so that it has begun to look like a Florida retirement community.

Fewer farmers are able to purchase the farms that are placed on the market by those who wish to retire. Consequently, land prices are depressed. Large corporations with highly mechanized operations are purchasing the land and replacing the small family farms with factorylike operations.

These changes are seriously affecting the ministry of High Plains Church. There are not as many people to fill the pews as there once was. Those who do attend have difficulty supporting the congregation financially because of poor economic times. The congregation has to carry on a constant struggle to pay the pastor's salary, maintain its small Sunday school, and cover the utility bills to keep the doors of the church open.

The enthusiasm that was once the hallmark of the congregation is being replaced by despair. The people are afraid that High Plains Church may cease to exist. They fear that they might lose what they have worked so hard to build up, and that something that has been an important part of their lives might be taken from them.

The survival of the congregation is a topic that frequently surfaces in the conversation of the members. During one of these conversations, a member shared what was happening at the congregation his daughter attended. "They're growing by leaps and bounds," he said. "The congregation is located on the edge of the city. They used to be dying with about seventy people gathering to worship on Sunday morning in a sanctuary that could seat four hundred. Now the sanctuary is packed and they are talking about two services."

"What happened to make them grow so fast?" asked one of the people in the group.

"I can't tell you for sure," came the reply. "My daughter thinks it's the evangelism program they're using. They sent their pastor to a large congregation in California to learn about a special evangelism program. When the pastor returned, she trained the members of the congregation to do evangelism visits. They've been growing ever since."

"Maybe we should send our pastor to California so he can learn about this program," another member of the group suggested.

"You know, that may not be a bad idea," a third person responded.

Within a few weeks, they obtained brochures that explained the program. The idea of sending the pastor off to California was considered at the next council meeting. Most of the council members had discussed it before over coffee and sweet rolls at the local restaurant and had already decided it was a great idea. The pastor did not object. "I'll try anything to help this congregation," he said. So, without further hesitation, the council voted unanimously to try the new evangelism program.

A special offering was taken at the next two worship services to help defray the cost. Once the program was explained to the other members of the congregation, they became excited and gave generously. It was not long before the pastor was winging his way to southern California to attend the program.

Two weeks later the excited pastor returned to the congregation. "There is so much potential for the program," he exclaimed, "this will really make a difference!"

Evangelism classes were soon formed and training began. However, as people began to learn more about the program, their support for it started to waver.

During one class, when the pastor was introducing the format of the evangelism visit, one member stopped him short. "You mean I've got to go up to my neighbor and ask him what would happen to his soul if he died tonight?" he asked. "I can't do that!"

Other members examined the program and decided they did not have the gifts to make evangelism visits. They thought several other members of the congregation were better suited to participate in the program.

A few members did complete the training and made visits for six months, but they did not receive a strong response from the people whom they visited. They became discouraged. There was no marked increase in attendance at High Plains. Within nine months the evangelism program was shelved and the people returned to their worries about the survival of their congregation.

High Plains Church followed a pattern that is characteristic of many congregations. (1) The congregation receives a stimulus from the outside that motivates them to become involved in evangelism. (2) The congregation seeks to become evangelistic in the quickest and easiest manner possible. With this criterion, "canned" programs are often viewed as the best solution. The results of these programs are highlighted by sales brochures and company representatives in order to raise the expectations of the congregation and obtain sales. The efforts needed to achieve those results are hidden or downplayed. The congregation receives the impression, therefore, that tremendous gain can be attained with little pain. (3) The program is initiated in the congregation, but the congregation is unprepared for the demands of the program and unwilling to meet those demands. (4) The congregation withdraws its support and the program dies an inglorious death. (5) The congregation returns to its search for a quick and easy solution to the "evangelism problem" or falls into depression and despair over its inability to become evangelistic.

Thankfully, there are other ways for congregations to become excited about and involved in evangelism. The tools to inspire this excitement and involvement already exist within every community of faith.

Evangelism begins when the people of God are motivated to proclaim the gospel of Jesus Christ. Motivation comes from two different sources: from the outside or from the inside.

The congregation of High Plains Church responded to outside forces. The members would have been content to continue with the status quo, but they could not. They were faced with dwindling attendance and tight finances. These factors persuaded them that they needed to become evangelistic and pushed them into action.

Everyone knows what it is like to be forced to do something. It is not a pleasant experience. People do what is expected of them, but they do it unwillingly. As soon as the outside motivation is lessened or removed, their behavior returns to what it was previously. The same is true of congregations.

Not only is outside motivation short term, but it motivates people and congregations toward the wrong goals.

The congregation of High Plains Church was not motivated
to become evangelistic because they had encountered a living
God and were excited about God's presence in their lives.
They wanted to reach out to people so that they could drag
them into their congregation, bolster their attendance figures, and improve their finances. While such goals may be
appropriate for corporate America, they have no place in the
congregation.

Inactive church members and the unchurched do not
respond in a positive manner to congregations driven by outside forces. Although the reasons may not be explicitly stated,
people can sense the motivation for a contact, conversation,
or invitation. A congregational member may say, "Hi, if you
don't have a church we'd like you to consider ours." However,
if he or she is driven by outside forces, the other person hears,
"Would you please come to our church? Our attendance is
falling off and we need more people to make our worship
service more comfortable and to make us look better when
we compare ourselves with other congregations."

A mere "We sure have missed you at church" uttered
to an inactive member is translated, "We sure miss your offering. Don't you know that finances are tight? If you don't
come, at least send your money."

What the inactive and unchurched do not sense in
such contacts are love and concern. They perceive, quite cor-
rectly, that they are not being approached for their own
benefit. Help with their personal struggles and ministry to
their needs is not the primary issue. Rather, they are being
asked to assist an organization of which they are not a part
or serve an institution from which they feel alienated.

The love and concern that are vital to any congregational program, especially evangelism, grow only out of
inner motivation. This motivation comes through an encounter with God's Word. The preaching and teaching of God's
Word are the greatest tools any congregation has to build a

strong sense of mission and to establish effective evangelistic programs and practices.

God's Word is powerful. It has the ability to change lives. Change takes place in people when they have the revelation that God personally loves them and is intimately involved in their lives. Overwhelmed by God's love, they see the world from a different perspective. They envision their lives as having a different purpose and conceive different goals for themselves and different paths to walk.

**God's Word is powerful.
It has the ability to change lives.
Change takes place in people
when they have the revelation that
God personally loves them and is
intimately involved in their lives.**

People who encounter God's Word in a fresh manner are filled with a contagious excitement. They want to share what has been revealed to them with everyone they meet. They become evangelists.

Something good has happened to these people. When they encounter others at work, at home, or during their leisure activities, they want to share their experience so that other people can have a similar experience. The drive of these new evangelists can at times be overwhelming, especially when it carries them to extremes. Yet on the whole, the people who are outside the church are receptive to their witness. They do not perceive the witness as an attempt to sell the institution of the church or as an appeal motivated for the benefit of the church. They see the witness as being genuinely motivated by love and concern for them.

Is not this every preacher's dream, to have an entire congregation encounter God through the sermon, become excited about their faith and set on fire by the Holy Spirit? It is this dream and faith in the power of God that keep preachers climbing into the pulpit to proclaim the Word of God. They discipline themselves to proclaim God's Word even when it appears that no one is listening, that no one cares, and that no changes are taking place.

Reality may never fulfill the dreams of preachers. Congregational members may never dance in the aisles of the church, or rush out the church doors to conquer the world for Jesus Christ, or sell all that they have and give it to the poor. Still, members of the congregation do encounter God. These are usually short encounters that take place over a long period of time. They change the lives of people in bits and pieces. They excite people over little truths and specific ideas. Slowly yet surely, these encounters with God transform the members of the congregation into God's image and the body of Christ.

The preaching and teaching of God's Word are the exact opposites of a "quick fix." It takes time, persistence, and a consistent proclaiming of God's Word to effect change, but the level of motivation achieved this way is deeper and longer lasting.

People not only respond to the gospel, they also respond to the call of God contained in the Scriptures. Both of these facets of the Christian message need to be preached and taught in order to motivate the congregation toward evangelism.

God's call in many ways is like looking into a mirror. When we hear God's call we see the person God desires us to be. At the same time we see who we truly are. It is often not a pleasant sight. We see our sinfulness—the times we have disobeyed God, the times we have been blind to the needs of others, and the times that we have been quiet and silently denied the Lord. The image that we behold drives us into the arms of a loving and forgiving God. Holding us close,

God speaks a word of forgiveness to our hearts and empowers us with the Spirit to change and to sin no more.

God's call in the areas of evangelism and personal witness is not often addressed in sermons and Bible studies. Some people observe that these topics have been replaced by concern for church budgets and the proclamation of sacrificial giving. Others feel that there are more pressing needs, such as examining God's movement through the sacraments or addressing the moral decay of our society. These are important topics, but to deal with them while ignoring the areas of personal witness and evangelism skews God's call and creates an imbalance in the Christian message.

Many pastors are uncomfortable dealing with the call of God in their Sunday morning sermons. They argue that the hardships of life, such as individual failure, broken relationships, and personal stress, are experienced to such a great extent on a daily basis that people do not need to be challenged during a worship service. Their prescription for the needs of the people they serve is to proclaim the love, compassion, and commitment of God. Certainly, all people need to hear these truths, yet to proclaim them exclusively alters God's message to God's people. People do not have the opportunity to see themselves in the mirror. They do not realize that God calls and empowers them to be more than who they are. They do not see their need to open themselves to the life-changing power of God's Spirit in their lives.

Change takes place in both the congregation as a whole and in the lives of the individual members when people see the discrepancies between the way things are and the way things should be. These discrepancies are highlighted as God's Word enlightens the minds and hearts of the people through preaching and teaching.

Sermons are wonderful opportunities to share God's call to be evangelists with the members of the congregation in the context of the whole Christian message. A skillfully crafted sermon can be effective in inspiring change. One rural pastor used the stories of historical figures to address the issues of evangelism and personal witness in his congregations. One Sunday each month he chose a person from history whose work would be commemorated that month in his denomination's calendar. He examined how that person struggled with the call of God in his or her life and the manner in which that person became a strong witness to the gospel of Jesus Christ. His emphasis was that a real person (not some great saint) encountered a living God and was changed. In response to the gospel, that person set about to accomplish specific and attainable tasks in order to share God's Word. These accomplishments, as small or as great as they were, touched people's lives and changed the world. These sermons helped the members of the congregation comprehend that God's call was to them and they could accomplish that to which God was calling them.

Another pastor made frequent references in his sermons to the candle given to each child at baptism. He pointed out that from the moment of their baptism God's people become lights to the world. Their lights shine as they speak God's Word and minister to the people around them. These references to the baptismal candle were woven into his sermons, but they were never the main topic. Through repetition, the members of the congregation began to see both the gifts and the call that are contained in baptism. This vision inspired several changes in the congregation.

Disgusted at the constant excuses congregational members gave for avoiding personal evangelism, one pastor developed a sermon series entitled, "Great Excuses of the Bible." He talked about the excuses offered by biblical characters when they were confronted by God. He dealt with Moses' excuse, "I can't speak very well," and Jeremiah's, "I'm too young," among others. This sermon series allowed the members of the congregation to see the biblical characters in a more human light and also enabled them to realize that excuses do not turn aside the call of God. The congregation was not changed overnight, but these sermons opened up the topic of evangelism and gave the congregation the opportunity to discuss the various excuses they had been using to avoid changing the status quo.

Along with sermons and Bible studies are other outstanding materials and programs that deal with the subject of evangelism and highlight God's call. Several excellent resources stress evangelism and deepen the participants' understanding of God's Word. *Witness to the World*, a twenty-session series, is an exciting and intriguing study of the Scripture.[1] Its purpose is to help congregations examine God's call to evangelism. Another thought-provoking work, written by Patrick Keifert, is entitled *Welcoming the Stranger: A Public Theology of Worship and Evangelism*.[2] It investigates congregational hospitality as expressed in the worship experience. Edward Marquardt's study, *Witnesses for Christ*,[3] is an effective means of helping members of the congregation witness more effectively. It offers many practical and insightful observations that empower and encourage personal witness.

It is not necessary for Bible studies to be specifically directed at the topic of evangelism in order for them to encourage evangelism. Studies done in the early 1980s by the Adult Christian Education Foundation (the Bethel Bible Study Series people) showed that participants in a comprehensive Bible study such as *The Bethel Series*, *Crossways!*, or *Search*[4] were more likely to articulate their faith. This stands to reason because one of the most frequently stated excuses by congregational members for avoiding a personal witness to others is a lack of biblical knowledge. These comprehensive Bible studies accomplish two tasks. They assist the participants to become more familiar with Scripture and motivate them to become more evangelistic in their words and style of life.

A congregational checklist is another useful tool to help the congregation discover the discrepancy between what they preach and what they practice.

A pastor of a congregation in a small Illinois town used a checklist (similar to the one found in the Appendix of this book) to stimulate his congregation and enable them to envision what evangelism could be in their congregation.

A congregational checklist is another useful tool to help the congregation discover the discrepancy between what they preach and what they practice.

The congregation had become complacent. They were not growing in membership, nor were they declining. The attendance was adequate, they were meeting their bills, and they had a well-attended Sunday school. The people felt that they were doing all that needed to be done.

The attitude of the congregation was disturbing to the pastor. He was pleased with many of the activities in the congregation, but he felt that the congregation fell far short of perfection. Things could be improved. Yet whenever he proposed a change, he met a stone wall. "Things are going just fine," he was told, "there is no need for change."

The pastor knew something needed to be done when he received a letter from a recent visitor to the congregation. The visitor had attended a Sunday morning worship service in search of a church home. During her visit she stated that no one from the congregation greeted her or acknowledged her presence. She took a cup of coffee during the fellowship period and waited for someone to visit with her, but no one did. The visitor's letter closed with the comment that she left the church that Sunday angry and vowed that she would never return.

The pastor did not share the letter itself with the church council. He knew that they would slough it off with the comment that "you win some and lose some." Instead, he devised a congregational checklist. During the next council meeting, he gave a copy of the checklist to each council member. Then he led them through the church with the instructions that they were to play the role of a first-time visitor. They even conducted a short worship service so that the council members could understand how a visitor felt on Sunday morning.

The members of the church council were disturbed by what they found. They had always imagined themselves to be a welcoming congregation. They discovered, however, that there were no signs in the building to direct visitors to offices, classrooms, or rest rooms. As they played the role of ushers and visitors, they noticed that the ushers were not particularly friendly or helpful. Because the pastor had led them through a worship service different from the one to which they were accustomed, they felt the service was uncomfortable and confusing. To say the least, they had a lively discussion for the remainder of the council meeting. By the end of the evening, all the council committees had specific suggestions to explore and implement.

To keep up the momentum for change in the congregation, the pastor led the women's Bible study circles and the members of the adult forum through a similar experience. They were equally disturbed and through their discussion they came up with additional ideas for study and change.

The complacency of the congregation was eliminated. As changes were implemented in the following months, the congregation evolved into a fellowship of God's people who were very aware of the manner in which they presented themselves to people outside of the church and who were very intentional in their outreach and welcoming of visitors.

A congregational checklist underscores an important truth in evangelism: Evangelism is not some program or activity that is announced on the congregational calendar with a note saying, "EVANGELISM, 7:00 WEDNESDAY." Evangelism is not just visiting the inactive church member or knocking on the door of a family who has recently moved into the neighborhood. Evangelism is the purpose of every meeting, worship service, and activity that is held within a congregation. Evangelism is woven into the fabric of congregational life. It cannot be separated from the fabric without destroying the material because it is not merely a design imprinted on the surface.

Evangelism is the purpose of every meeting, worship service, and activity that is held within a congregation. Evangelism is woven into the fabric of congregational life.

Dr. Kennon Callahan, in his book *Twelve Keys to an Effective Church*,[5] identifies twelve areas of congregational life that need to be well developed if the congregation is to accomplish the mission to which it is called. If the mission of the church is to proclaim the gospel of Jesus Christ, to be evangelical, then the effective church is also an evangelistic church. These twelve areas are (1) specific, concrete missional objectives, (2) pastoral and lay visitation, (3) dynamic corporate worship, (4) significant relational groups, (5) strong leadership resources, (6) streamlined structure and participatory decision making, (7) several competent programs and activities, (8) open accessibility, (9) high visibility, (10) adequate parking, land, and landscaping, (11) adequate space and facilities within the building, and (12) solid financial resources.

Meeting these criteria is a daunting task for any congregation, especially a rural one, but they are not insurmountable goals. With persistence, planning, and prayer, congregations can strive to develop these key elements. It is not necessary for all of these key elements to be in place before a congregation can consider itself evangelistic. Each one contributes to the mission of the congregation. Dr. Callahan states that the congregation should focus on the elements in which it is strongest and seek to improve them. Then the congregation should selectively turn its attention to the other elements.[6]

The sermon, the Bible study, and the congregational checklist are all tools that can be used to motivate the members of rural congregations to become more intentional in their evangelism and personal witness. A final tool is the role model.

An often neglected truth is that the real experts in rural ministry and evangelism are rural pastors. They are the ones who live in the rural community and who experience the joy and the sorrow, the pain and the tears of the rural people. Rural pastors understand most clearly what grief rural communities are enduring and what challenges they face. They do not need to travel thousands of miles and develop intricate and sophisticated programs like other so-called experts.

Many of these rural ministry and evangelism experts have developed programs within their congregations that effectively minister to the needs of the people and proclaim the gospel of Jesus Christ to those outside of the church. People who are concerned about rural ministry and evangelism often need to look only down the road a few miles to discover something that would be helpful for their own congregation.

The pastor of High Plains Church discovered this truth after the "Great Evangelism Program Fiasco." While talking to colleagues at a local pastors' meeting, he discovered that a pastor in a community only thirty miles away had developed a helpful greeter-visitor program for his congregation. Over coffee and donuts, the High Plains pastor determined that this program could be useful in helping his congregation become a more welcoming church that cared for its visitors. Several other pastors recommended a new Bible study from a small publisher. The pastor decided that he would take a look at the study and possibly offer it to his congregation in the spring.

In addition to being an abundant and inexpensive source of ideas, programs developed by rural pastors are often in locations near enough that the members of another congregation can experience them on a firsthand basis. Representatives of the congregation can examine the role model and determine from their experience and conversations with pastors and members of the modeling congregation whether the program would be appropriate in their own situation. A pastor might also direct the attention of his or her congregation to what the modeling congregation is doing and tactfully say, "See what that congregation is doing. If they can do that, we can too!" Such direct exposure to ideas motivates the congregation toward evangelism.

It may be pleasant to dream of quick fixes and magic wands, but in the real world of rural ministry they are only a dream. Thankfully, the rural pastor and congregation have powerful gifts and tools at their disposal that can be used to inspire change and evangelism. The tools of preaching, teaching, self-examination, and learning from others are common and well worn, but they are no less effective. God's Spirit uses them to produce changes and empower people beyond our wildest dreams and the limits of our faith.

Discussion Questions

1. How have sermons and Bible studies in your congregation addressed the topic of evangelism in the past?

2. How can the sermons and Bible studies address the topic of evangelism in the future?

3. What specific issues in the areas of evangelism and personal witness need to be addressed in your congregation? (For example, congregational cliques, lack of biblical knowledge.)

4. In what key elements is your congregation strong? How can these elements be further developed?

5. What is the most important key element that needs to be developed in your congregation?

6. What role models do you have for evangelism and personal witness?

Notes

1. Dennis Anderson, Mary Hughes, Lynn Nakamura, Mark Powell, and Walter Taylor, *Witness to the World* (Minneapolis: Augsburg Fortress, 1991).

2. Patrick Keifert, *Welcoming the Stranger: A Public Theology of Worship and Evangelism* (Minneapolis: Augsburg Fortress, 1992).

3. Edward Marquardt, *Witnesses for Christ* (Minneapolis: Augsburg, 1981).

4. *The Bethel Series* (Madison: Adult Christian Education Foundation, 1981); *Crossways!* (Minneapolis: Crossways International, 1984); *Search* (Minneapolis: Augsburg, 1985).

5. Kennon Callahan, *Twelve Keys to an Effective Church* (San Francisco: Harper & Row, 1983), xiii.

6. Ibid., xvi.

6
Living in the Past or Striving for the Future

*This one thing I do:
forgetting what lies behind and
straining forward to what lies
ahead, I press on toward the goal
for the prize of the heavenly call
of God in Christ Jesus.
(Phil. 3:13-14)*

Young Sarah Miller was eleven months old. Being an above-average child, at least in the eyes of her parents and grandparents, she had mastered the art of crawling several months ago. Now, Sarah had set her sights on greater horizons. Sarah wanted to walk.

For three weeks, Sarah had been preparing for her new venture. She would crawl over to the sofa and pull herself up onto her feet. Holding firmly to the cushions, Sarah would travel the entire length of the sofa, first in one direction and then in the other. She would become tired of the sofa after five or ten minutes and then direct her attention to the coffee table—an island of excitement in the vast ocean of the living room. Nudging herself around so that her back was to the sofa and she faced the coffee table, Sarah would take one sliding step and throw herself at the table. She would catch the edge of the table with the upper part of her body, then right herself and waddle around the coffee table, exploring its every nook and cranny. Sarah was the queen of this vast domain, and all her subjects except for a rebellious older brother would clap and shout her praises.

Sarah knew the coffee table intimately. She had perfected her sidestep through hours of practice and judged herself ready to expand the borders of her empire. Sarah came to the edge of the coffee table and stopped. Instead of taking the familiar corner, she turned her body and pointed herself toward her dad. He, seeing the gleam in her eye, understood the significance of the moment. Reaching his arms toward her, he began to chant, "Come to Daddy, come to Daddy."

Sarah's heart began to race as she worked up her courage. Her father's chant had attracted the attention of her mother, who joined in with her words of encouragement, "Come on Sarah, you can do it!"

The time had come. Sarah lifted her foot and took one step forward. For a brief moment she wobbled, unsure of what to do next. Her hesitancy became her downfall. Not being used to her full weight, her legs crumpled. Sarah's body pitched forward and she tumbled to the floor. Tears of frustration came to her eyes and a wail of surprise came from her mouth.

Her father scooped Sarah up in his arms and comforted her. He placed her beside the coffee table and encouraged her to try again. She did try, but to no avail. Each time she would crash down to the carpet.

Sarah did not walk that day, yet her parents did not take her aside and counsel her not to try again. Sarah did not encounter warning protests of, "No, honey, don't try to walk again, you'll never be able to do it," when she turned from the coffee table and attempted to negotiate the distance between it and the chair. Everyone knew that with enough time and persistence, Sarah would walk.

Unfortunately, the rural congregation does not usually receive this kind of encouraging reaction when it attempts its first feeble steps at evangelism.

Bethany Church was dead in the water. At least that is what its pastor, John Clemmons, believed. The people came to worship on Sunday morning and held a Sunday school for the children. A few adults attended a Bible study on Tuesday evenings, the women's group met twice a month, and the council met the second Thursday of the month. That was it. There was no interest in regional or churchwide programs. There was no support for world and home missions or efforts in the area of evangelism. This situation was disturbing to John, but what disturbed him even more was the fact that the members of the congregation appeared content and complacent.

John decided that something needed to be done. At the monthly council meeting, he proposed that the congregation conduct an every-member visitation program. The purpose of the visit would not be to solicit money. Rather, it would give the members an opportunity to talk about their congregation and share their ideas about what they would like to see happen. John hoped that the visits would not only give the people the opportunity to share but also stir up a little excitement and enthusiasm within the congregation. John's proposal met with immediate disapproval.

"Sounds like a lot of work to me, Pastor," the council president responded. "Maybe we can have the members fill out a questionnaire after a worship service instead."

"I don't think an every-member visit will work," objected another council member. "They tried that at Our Redeemer's a few years ago and the people really got upset. They didn't like people coming into their homes to talk about the church. Some members even threatened to quit the church."

"I think we have already tried an every-member visit," a third member thought aloud. "It must have been about fifteen years ago when Pastor Damler was here. . . . I don't think that it worked then. It probably won't work now."

A great deal of time and effort on John's part and on the part of some dedicated members of the congregation was needed to spur the people of Bethany to take their first faltering steps in evangelism. It was much more difficult than encouraging a small child to walk.

One wonders what it is that makes a congregation so resistant to new ideas and possibilities. Good-natured, fun-loving, committed people begin to take on the characteristics of stubborn mules when confronted by something new. Upon reflection, one realizes that what causes the people to respond in this manner is fear. Fear is the greatest threat to any evangelism proposal—or any other new idea. Fear constrains the rural congregation, hinders its faith, and robs it of its power. Surrounded by their fears, congregations become like small children who huddle under their blankets at night to hide from the monsters that stalk them in the dark.

One of the greatest fears that rural congregations have is that of failure. Failure projects a powerful image in our society. Most of the time, failure carries negative connotations and is avoided at all costs. People do not want to think of themselves as failures; they want to be successes. They are attracted to the winners and the successful around them but repelled by the losers and the failures.

In addition to this cultural image of failure, people in rural communities have had to face a great deal of actual failure. Farms have been lost, living standards have fallen, and society's attention has turned away from rural areas toward urban communities, thus denigrating rural life. Surrounded by failure, rural congregations view any new idea as another way to fail rather than as a fresh opportunity to succeed.

As individuals congregations need to confess their sins and receive forgiveness through the cross of Christ, and as a community of believers they need to do the same.

A deeper issue associated with failure is that failure confronts the congregation with the stark reality that it is a human institution. Congregations tend to see themselves through rose-colored lenses. They think of themselves as always warm and friendly, never cold and cliquish. They are always loving and forgiving, never hateful and judgmental. Congregations do not have arguments, they have discussions; and there are never any politics in congregations, some people are simply more persuasive than others.

Failure takes away the congregation's rose-colored lenses and reminds them that no matter how hard they try, they will never be able to follow the Lord perfectly. At times, failure enables the congregation to see that God has not yet finished molding them into God's image. This recognition can be distressing for a body of believers who desire to be complete and whole. Failure may also confront the congregation with the truth that they are sinful and unclean. As individuals they need to confess their sins and receive forgiveness through the cross of Christ, and as a community of believers they need to do the same. Such a truth should not pose a difficulty to Christians who hear on a regular basis that Jesus died for the sins of humankind, but even so they struggle to deal with their sinfulness and need for forgiveness.

Literally hundreds of fears confront rural congregations besides the fear of failure. Some of the concerns are valid while others border on paranoia. Big or small, these fears have the potential to paralyze a congregation so that any evangelism endeavor becomes difficult if not impossible.

A common fear is that someone will be offended by the proposed activity. This was one of the fears that Pastor Clemmons faced at Bethany. It is a valid fear. The purpose of any evangelism activity is to reach out to people and invite them to become members of God's family and involve them in the activities of the congregation. It is counterproductive to do something that offends people and drives them further from the congregation and from faith in Jesus Christ.

Often the very mention of this fear ends any further discussion. No one who loves others and is concerned about their welfare wants to take such a risk. Yet, in many instances this fear is unreasonable. The fact that one person was offended may conceal the reality that four or five other people became involved in the congregation through the same activity. The fear stems from a desire for an unattainable perfection, from a hope not to offend anyone. Yet, as Abraham Lincoln once said, "You cannot please all of the people all of the time." The gifts of communication, confession, and forgiveness were given to be used in situations where people are unintentionally offended.

Fear of offending someone also can keep congregations from learning from their mistakes. If the congregation can discover why people were offended previously, they can then modify the activity to prevent a recurrence.

Another common fear is that the congregation will be unable to afford the proposed activity. It is not unusual for a church treasurer to sit passively while the rest of the council members debate a proposed course of action. Then just before the vote is taken, the treasurer will point out that offerings have been down for the last two months, there is only a balance of $2.95 in the checkbook, and there is no way that the congregation will be able to pay for the program. After the treasurer speaks, a vote is not even needed. Defeat is inevitable.

**To break the bonds of
fears, it is necessary for the
pastor and the congregational
leadership to refocus the attention
of the people.**

Fiscal responsibility is indeed necessary in any rural congregation. Yet, financial fears can take on the tone of Chicken Little announcing that the sky is falling. This fear denies the reality that the people of God will support programs that they believe in and know to be effective. It also rejects the truth that God will provide for the people of God as they seek to be obedient to the will of God.

These fears and countless others have the common link of being focused on the past. The reasoning goes like this: If people have been offended in the past, they will be offended in the future; or, if we have not been able to afford something in the past, we will not be able to afford it in the future. The assertion is made that the future will simply be a repeat of the past. To break the bonds of fears, it is necessary for the pastor and the congregational leadership to refocus the attention of the people.

They can draw attention to the changes that can be made to bring about a different result. Perhaps people have been offended in the past, but specific changes in the program will be made that will lessen the possibility of offense and increase the effectiveness of the program. It may be true that in the past the congregation was unable to afford the program, but a special fund drive will be started and matching gifts will be sought. The past need not be repeated in the future.

The pastor may help the congregation confront their fears by asking them to imagine a worst-case scenario. If the change is adopted, what is the worst that can happen? It may be realistic to expect that one or two members of the congregation may become upset and threaten to leave, but the entire congregation will not walk out the door. Neither is such a circumstance entirely negative. This situation might afford congregational leaders the opportunity to converse with the upset member(s) about the call of God to the individual and congregation. Such a dialogue could be helpful to all the parties involved.

The congregation may fall short in its fund drive. This does not mean that the congregation will be forced to file for bankruptcy. It may only mean that the evangelism program will need to be modified to fit the funds that are raised, or that other sources for funding will need to be investigated. Gloom, doom, and disaster are rarely realistic scenarios for evangelism activities.

Role models are another effective way of turning the attention of rural congregations from the past to the future. Unless the congregation is the front-runner in an area, it is likely that other congregations have already done what the congregation wishes to accomplish. The experience of such congregations can be used to inspire the imagination of the congregational members and enable them to realize what they can do.

No one who puts
a hand to the plow and looks back
is fit for the kingdom of God.
(Luke 9:62)

Followers of Jesus have been trapped in the past before. Luke addresses this issue when he writes about three predecessors of the reluctant congregational member (Luke 9:57-62). People were attracted to Jesus and wanted to follow him. To one who offered to follow him, Jesus responded that there would be no worldly security for any who followed him. Jesus asked another man to follow him, but the man replied that he first had to bury his father. A third man wanted to follow Jesus but wanted to say good-bye to his family before he left. Jesus addressed these responses by saying, "No one who puts a hand to the plow and looks back is fit for the kingdom of God" (9:62).

This statement of Jesus seems harsh, but it stresses the truth that to follow Jesus means that people must shed the temptation to live in the past. God's call redirects the focus of God's people from the past to the person of God. When they behold God's power and glory, God's people can walk together with God along the path that leads to the future.

One benefit of the past is that we can learn from it if we ask the right questions. This is not as easy as it first appears.

John Clemmons of Bethany Church was tempted to react to the rejection of his proposal by the church council with despair. "Why doesn't God ever allow anything to be easy?" he asked himself. This question was followed by a host of others such as, "What's wrong with those people? What have I done to deserve such an obstinate council? Why do things like this always happen to me?"

These are dead-end questions. They do not lead to an understanding of the situation nor do they open the way for a solution to the problem. Yet, they are questions we commonly ask when our expectations are not met.

It is not difficult for a rural congregation to become bogged down by asking itself similar questions of despair. These questions have no answers, yet the congregation continues trying to find answers by asking them over and over again. Each time an answer is not found, despair and frustration grow. Eventually the despair and frustration become so great that the congregation flees from the challenge and takes refuge in the status quo. There the questions are silenced, and the people feel secure again, convinced that any change, especially evangelism, is not possible for them.

John Clemmons did not fall into this trap. When he caught himself asking himself these questions, he realized what he was doing. He changed his behavior and began to pose constructive questions that enabled him to find solutions to the challenge that confronted him. He had learned these questions in a personal development course he had taken.[1]

The first question John asked was, "*What is good about this, or could be good about this situation?*" Obstacles and challenges are almost always looked upon negatively by congregations. They are thought to slow the congregation down, hinder it from reaching its goal, or prevent it from fulfilling its vision. This perspective stresses that the benefit of the change or the activity is contained only in its accomplishment. This is rarely the case.

The ultimate challenge that confronts rural congregations is to proclaim the gospel of Jesus Christ by reaching out to the unchurched of their community to invite them to participate in a relationship with God. It will be a wonderful day when this goal is reached. Until that time, the rural congregation can benefit from the process of striving for that goal. Members of the congregation may need to increase their understanding of the Scriptures, discover and develop their unique individual talents and gifts, and learn how to work together as the body of Christ. All of these are advantages for the congregation that strives to reach the goal of evangelizing the community. There are similar benefits for the congregation as it attempts to overcome smaller obstacles and meet the everyday challenges that confront it. The question, "What is good about this, or could be good about this situation?" focuses on this truth.

People have little control
over others, yet they have a great
amount of control over
themselves. They cannot easily
force other people to change,
but they can change themselves.

The second question is, *"What is not yet proper or right?"* This question focuses on the fact that modifications and alterations can always be made to allow the congregation to reach its goal. The congregation is never trapped and it is not powerless against the outside forces it confronts. As the congregation travels the road of evangelism and mission, it may find it necessary to make detours and change lanes in order to achieve its vision. It is within the congregation's ability to take these actions and continue in its evangelism endeavors.

Another helpful question that John asked himself was, *"What am I willing to do to make it the way I want it?"* This question reminded John that if the goal were to be accomplished, he would have to make changes in his life and doing so would take personal effort. In answer to his question, John determined that he would need to do some further research on every-member visitation programs and that he would need to discuss his research individually with each member of the council.

A favorite game of congregations, councils, and committees is "pass the buck." If a goal is not reached or if a program flops, it is always someone else's fault. This reasoning not only gets the individual or group off the hook, it assures them that they need not do anything further to achieve the goal. The problem is someone else's responsibility.

People have little control over others, yet they have a great amount of control over themselves. They cannot easily force other people to change, but they can change themselves. The question, "What am *I* willing to do?" concentrates the attention of the individual or group upon themselves. It is in their own lives that the possibility for change is the greatest.

"What am I willing to stop doing to make it the way I want it?" is the fourth question. This question brings with it the understanding that there are times when we are our own worst enemies. There are times when people hedge their bets. They will say something like, "Well, if this program doesn't work, that's OK. We'll just try something else." Their lack of total support and commitment fails to inspire people and may cause the other people to question the vision. At other times, a person may become so caught up in a project that he or she pushes other people too hard. People respond to nagging by digging in their heels and sabotaging the project.

The question also reminds individuals and congregations that Christians do not have endless amounts of time and money. People tend to take on additional projects and attempt to carry them along with everything else in their lives.

The result is a hectic lifestyle where one achieves only limited, and possibly unfulfilling, success in a variety of areas. In reality, if something is going to be added to one's life, then it will be necessary to remove something else. Rather than take one more evening away from the family, it may be better to resign from a second committee or drop a recreational activity. This deliberate choice can only be made when individuals or the congregation ask this question and establish priorities in their lives.

The fifth question is the most challenging one to answer: *"How can I do what's necessary to get the job done and enjoy doing it?"* No one likes to be forced to do anything. When one *must* do something, that activity becomes a task or a chore. It exists on the same level as taking out the garbage, changing diapers, or cleaning eave troughs.

Evangelism was given to the church by God as a privilege. It is a fulfilling and meaningful activity. It was never meant to be a chore. Yet, congregations have done a great job in making it a task. The evangelism committee is forced to visit inactive members of the congregation because no one else will do it and it is something that everyone in the congregation feels has to be done. People are forced to stand in the entryway of the church and shake hands with people when they would much rather quietly sit in their pew, because the congregation needs greeters.

It is not amazing that rural congregations engage in so few evangelism activities. What is amazing is that when members are faced with "have to" situations they continue to support any form of evangelism at all.

One way to turn evangelism from a task into an enjoyable activity is to take the time to match an individual's gifts with the activity at hand. Find outgoing and gregarious people to be the greeters. Discover people who like to visit and talk about the church and ask them to call on inactive or marginal members of the congregation. Train the quiet yet caring congregational member in techniques to share his or her faith in a one-to-one situation and to work on record keeping and behind-the-scene tasks.

It is also helpful to take the time to be creative in the approach to the evangelism endeavor.

John Clemmons had the task of researching every-member visitation programs and then sharing his findings with the members of his council. Rather than sit in the office and pore over the material, John decided to take advantage of the beautiful summer weather. He packed up a few books and magazine articles and headed to the beach. He was able to enjoy the children playing and feel the wind and warmth while gathering the information that he needed.

When it came time to share his research, John invited each member of his council to a light lunch at a local restaurant. John enjoyed conversations over a meal. He used the opportunity not only to talk about the every-member visitation plan but also to solicit the hopes and fears that each council member had in the area of evangelism. John was not the only one who enjoyed the occasion. The council members also enjoyed the meal and appreciated being spared a dry presentation during a council meeting. A little creativity and imagination on John's part turned a chore into a pleasant and enjoyable activity.

Freed from most of their fears and having learned from the past through the use of helpful questions, rural congregations are able to strive toward their visions of evangelism. Yet, the people of the congregation must be warned that the journey before them is not a short one. It is a journey that will last the rest of their lives and demand patience and persistence from them.

Often congregations are tricked into believing that an evangelism activity will bring quick results. This is hardly ever the case, especially in rural areas. If they believe that this is true, rural congregations quickly become disheartened and discouraged when results are not immediately forthcoming. The rural church scene is littered with abandoned programs and rusting evangelism activities that simply were not given enough time to produce results.

It may be necessary for the members of the congregation to remind themselves of God's persistence and patience in their lives. Many of them have experienced a roller-coaster ride in their relationship with God and with the church. Sometimes the relationship was close, sometimes it was distant. At times they were active and at other times inactive. Through it all, God's love remained constant. God continued to call them through the words of family, friends, and congregational members into a close, dynamic relationship. God persisted until they responded, and God still moves in their lives to draw them closer.

God's persistence and patience present a pattern that every rural congregation is challenged to copy. With persistence and patience the rural congregation can reach out, touch the lives of the people in its community, and be assured that the Holy Spirit will move and draw people into a fresh and living relationship with God.

Evangelism is not just for the large congregation or limited to the urban congregation. Rural congregations are called to proclaim the gospel of Jesus Christ and to be evangelical as well. This task is not impossible for rural congregations to achieve. Evangelism is an endeavor that takes informed leadership and a motivated membership. When these two elements combine in a rural congregation, that congregation becomes a shining light in the darkness of the world and a center of ministry that meets the needs of the people around it.

Discussion Questions

1. What are the fears that enslave the people in your congregation?

2. How can these fears be addressed and minimized?

3. What are some questions that you may find helpful in dealing with the situations and challenges that confront you and your congregation?

4. Have you prematurely given up on any one person, any group, or any activity? Are you able to do something different and try again?

Note

1. *Personal Power*, a tape series by Anthony Robbins (San Diego: Robbins Research International, 1989).

7
Just Down the Road

With toil and labor we worked night and day . . . in order to give you an example to imitate. (2 Thess. 3:8, 9)

B eing a Christian was something new, exciting, wonderful, and mysterious for the people in Thessalonica. They had responded to the message Paul had preached to them. They had openly repented of their sin and had been baptized. Then they began to walk the path called "the Christian life," although they were not sure where it went or how they were to travel along it. They were first-generation Christians—no one had traveled this path before them.

A dispute erupted in the congregation. Most of them believed that Jesus would return any day to establish his kingdom and gather his followers to be with him. However, they were divided over the question: "How does one wait for Jesus to return?" One side argued that it was best to quit their jobs and to occupy their time in prayer, Bible study, and theological discussion. The other side continued to work and soon found themselves supporting the other members of the congregation.

Paul intervened in the argument and blasted the lifestyle of the idle Christians. He did so, not with great theological arguments, but with his own life as an example. "Look at me," he exclaimed. "When I was with you I worked hard. If you want to know how a Christian should live, then follow my lead."

Role models are an important element in both personal and congregational lives. They enable people to visualize what is expected of them and what they are able to do. Role models help rural congregations understand they are able to engage in evangelistic activities that can be adapted to their particular situation.

Often rural congregations believe that only urban and suburban congregations are engaged in evangelism. This is not true. Literally hundreds of rural congregations have developed innovative programs and activities that proclaim the gospel of Jesus Christ. The following examples, taken from real life, are just a smattering of what can be found "just down the road" in rural America.

Operation Jonah

Operation Jonah is an evangelism project sponsored by six congregations that served a small Wisconsin town and the surrounding community. The participating congregations include a Seventh Day Baptist Church, a United Methodist Church, two Lutheran Churches, a Roman Catholic Church, and a nondenominational church. For several years these congregations have worked together in a variety of ecumenical activities. A community choir, joint youth activities, and special community worship services are just a few of these activities.

Role models are an important element in both personal and congregational lives. They enable people to visualize what is expected of them and what they are able to do.

It was during a gathering of the clergy that the topic of a community evangelism project was first discussed. However, the idea did not immediately take shape. It was a year before Operation Jonah was planned and initiated. It would be a communitywide effort to identify the unchurched, determine their needs, and invite them to participate in one of the congregations.

The first major task faced by the congregations was to develop a mission statement. Several theological issues were addressed in this process. The participants discovered there were fewer barriers to the common goal of proclaiming the gospel of Jesus Christ than they first thought. This dialogue strengthened the bonds between the congregations and increased the level of trust.

A group of women from the participating congregations came together after the mission statement had been developed. They were all longtime residents of the community and were familiar with the names and families of the area. Together they scoured the telephone book and identified approximately four hundred people whom they knew to be unchurched or whose affiliation they could not identify.

A brochure was developed and sent to each of these individuals. The brochure gave some basic information about the program and about the congregations involved in the endeavor. It also asked for a response from the individual and some information about his or her needs. Those people who did not reply were contacted by telephone by a volunteer.

As a result of the survey, sixty people requested more information about one of the congregations or a visit by a pastor. Several new families began attending worship services. Even before the brochure was sent, one man responded to a newspaper article that described what the congregations were doing. "I read the newspaper article about Operation Jonah and decided it was talking about me," he told a pastor. The man joined one of the congregations and his children became active in the Sunday school.

Operation Jonah was a creative way of reaching out to the unchurched in a rural community. It underscored the reality that not everyone in a rural community is associated with a congregation. Congregations discovered that they could be bound together by their common mission and pool their resources effectively to draw people into the family of God.

Liturgy Helpers

The members of St. Matthew's Lutheran Church have developed a caring way to assist the people who visit their worship services. They realized that their denominational liturgy is sometimes difficult and confusing for those who have not previously attended such a worship service. This unfamiliarity discourages visitors from returning and becoming involved in the congregation.

The congregation was concerned because several new people were visiting their services each week. St. Matthew's is located about twenty miles from Green Bay, Wisconsin. Their small community is beginning to experience change and growth due to the urban sprawl of Green Bay. The members of the congregation felt that it was essential for them to make the visitors to their worship services feel as welcome and comfortable as possible.

The pastor and congregation determined that the best solution to the situation was to train members of the congregation to assist visitors with the liturgy. They invited volunteers, and ten were chosen for training. These people were shown how to be hospitable and to make visitors feel welcome and were given more extensive information about the liturgy.

Now when a visitor drops by on Sunday morning, that person is greeted by a trained member of the congregation, who sits beside the visitor during the service and offers guidance if the guest has any difficulty. After the service the member introduces the guest to the pastor and perhaps other members of the congregation. The congregation of St. Matthew's has received positive feedback from this program, and many of the visitors have chosen to become a part of the congregation.

Guided by Needs

Some years ago eighty-five percent of the families in one community in the state of Washington were active in farming. A number of changes such as increased acreage per farm forced many of those families out of farming. The population of the town was decimated and the congregation of Grace Church was forced to examine seriously its mission. If the congregation did not change as the members grew older, it would inevitably become smaller. On the other hand, if changes could be made that would enable the congregation to reach out to the seventy-five to eighty percent of the population who were unchurched, the congregation had a potential for growth.

Led by their pastor, the congregation of Grace Church assessed the needs of their community. One of the needs they uncovered was religious education for the youth. The pastor designed a youth study program that allowed seventh- and eighth-grade students to ask the religious and personal questions that troubled them. Two or three young people from unchurched families often go through the program along with youth from Grace Church when it is offered. Their experience with the church often touches the lives of other members of their families. Several baptisms, both of adults and children, can be directly attributed to the youth program.

A teenage pregnancy sparked the formation of a weekly gathering of high school students called simply "Group." This gathering takes place at the school. It is a time for the young people to discuss real-life issues and struggle with the questions that confront them. The young people have discovered that the church is more than an institution of authority. They have realized that the church and the message it proclaims can empower them for life.

The community has few buildings in which organizations can meet. Organizations were dying or were not being formed because they could not find a suitable gathering place. In the midst of this situation stood the church with a building that was rarely occupied. The solution seemed obvious—allow the organizations to use the church building—but it was a difficult step for the congregation to take. Much prayer and persuasion were needed before the doors of the church were opened to support groups, scout troops, and 4-H clubs. Now strong ties are being formed between the congregation and the members of these organizations.

These changes made by the congregation of Grace Church have had an effect on both the congregation and the community. The congregation has discovered a new sense of mission and it has grown. This new focus on mission is reflected in a sentence the members frequently use to call themselves to action: "It's no penalty to be little, but with these gifts we dare not be small."

Spiritual Growth Leads to Outreach

When Pastor Dave Hermann interviewed for the call at St. Luke's and Calvary churches, he told the call committee that evangelism was not his forte. He preferred to focus on the spiritual growth of the congregation. Now, several years later, both he and the congregations have discovered that spiritual growth will automatically and necessarily lead outward. Outreach has become the next logical step in the spiritual journey of the congregation.

The population of the Minnesota town where St. Luke's is located has been declining for several years. Members of St. Luke's had moved to the far reaches of the United States, but most of them had never transferred their church membership. One of the first evangelistic steps the congregation took was to contact these distant members and encourage them to seek membership in congregations within the communities where they were presently living.

This first step was not an easy one for the congregation to take. Many felt that it was asking members to leave the church. Before sending the letters, the nature of the church was discussed in two church council meetings. The council realized through these discussions that church membership was more than having one's name on a roll, that it really involved activity in a congregation. The council then voted to send the letters to distant members. The letters did provoke some negative reactions, both from the members who had moved and from their families back at St. Luke's. Each time a question arose, it was used as an opportunity to explain the nature of the church to the congregation.

Several years after the letters were sent, this step was seen as very successful. Many people have transferred their membership and have become involved in other congregations. The congregation of St. Luke's celebrates each transfer, and those who move away from the area now transfer almost immediately because, as one member said, "They know this is important to the church."

The next step the congregation took was to reach out to absent members. The congregation intentionally did not use the term "inactive" because of its demeaning connotation. This step involved the implementation of a program called, "Who Cares Anyway?"[1]

The program involves five members of the congregation who meet with the pastor for a Bible study relating to the issue of absent members, how to communicate with them, and how to reinvolve them in the congregation. These people then select particular absent members whom they contact on a regular basis, seeking to show them caring behaviors and establish a closer relationship with them. Over time it is hoped that opportunities will develop where congregational activity and a renewed faith walk by the absent members can be encouraged.

This activity has met with modest success. Its implications for the church council and congregation, however, were significant. Suddenly the people felt that they were doing something about a problem that had been ignored for years.

Undergirding all of these activities is a strong Bible study program. When Pastor Hermann accepted the call to St. Luke's and Calvary there was no Bible study. Now adults gather every Wednesday evening and Sunday morning. One of the most helpful books the congregation has used is *Christian Caregiving* by Kenneth Haugk.[2] Study of the book has had a significant impact on the participants' lives because it has given them an opportunity to share their faith with their classmates and encouraged them to witness to people they know rather than to strangers or door-to-door. The original twenty-seven members of the Bible study have set the goal of involving fifteen to thirty more people in the class. With an average attendance of 150 at the worship service, this level of participation would mean that about one-third of the congregation would be involved in Bible study and evangelism activities.

Responding to the Changes

Covenant Church is located in a farming community of 1,500 people only ten minutes from Fresno, California. More than a hundred years old, the church was founded in 1888 by Danish settlers. In the late 1940s the congregation had an average worship attendance of 250. By 1983 this number had declined to 95. It was obvious to the members of the church that something needed to be done.

When the congregation examined their situation, several items caught their attention. First, it was apparent that because what they were presently doing was not working, change was needed. The congregation felt that the greatest opportunity for growth lay in asking friends and inactive members to become involved in congregational activities. The denominational book of worship was viewed as a deterrent to evangelism, and the church's traditional music was not thought to be attractive to the unchurched visitor. The congregation realized that they were doing little to socialize with visitors. Visitors would sit in the back of the sanctuary and leave immediately after the service. Finally, the congregation discovered that they had no identity in the community. Only the members of Covenant Church knew who they were and what they were about.

One of the first programs that the congregation began was a Hispanic worship service and Bible study. Although Danes were no longer settling in the area, the Hispanic population was growing rapidly. The congregation discovered this new worship service was the easiest program to implement. The Spanish worship service now has an average attendance of eighteen.

Changes were made to the existing worship service as well. The entire service was printed in a booklet so that it would be easier for the first-time visitor to follow. The music was altered to include songs that were easier to sing and could be used with guitar accompaniment. The preaching style became more conversational and educational. To entice members and visitors to linger after the service, coffee and cookies were served near the doors. These changes were difficult for the congregation to make, but by continually holding up the primary purpose of evangelizing non-Christian neighbors, they were able to make the changes. The average worship attendance now stands at 131.

To gain identity in the community, Covenant Church decided to sponsor a service project. The congregation began serving a Thursday noon lunch for 150 high school students as a sponsor of the Fellowship of Christian Athletes.

Expanding Worship and Mission

Memorial Church is a large congregation that finds itself challenged by ministry to its rural community in Iowa.

Yet, when the present pastors arrived at Memorial Church, the congregation did not have a strong direction to its ministry and only twenty-two percent of the congregation were worshiping on Sunday morning.

One of the most significant changes at Memorial Church was the development of an alternate form of worship. However, before any changes were made, the congregation involved itself in a study of the meaning and purpose of worship. This study enabled the membership to see that changes could be made without betraying or negating their denominational traditions.

They decided, as a result of the study, to try an alternate worship service at one of the two Sunday morning services. The service provides a variety of worship experiences. Guitars are sometimes used, but the organ is the primary instrument. A songbook entitled *The Other Song Book*[3] is used because it includes a variety of contemporary and traditional hymns. The liturgy is printed in the bulletin and visitors find that they can easily participate in the service. An increase in attendance of three percent is directly attributable to the alternate service.

Memorial Church has also stressed evangelism by becoming involved in community, national, and worldwide mission programs. The congregation has joined with other congregations in the town to provide several community worship services and a free supper program. This ecumenical group also provides the hospital lounge with a "Care Note" rack.[4] Memorial Church has also started a Christian preschool as an intentional ministry of the congregation.

To reach beyond the community, the members of Memorial sponsor a foreign missionary. They also became mission partners with a new congregation in Iowa and expanded their involvement in mission partnership by supporting the ministry of a congregation in California. These activities gave a fresh vision to the congregation and enabled the members to regain their sense of direction and purpose.

What has happened in the congregations described here shows that every rural congregation can be an evangelistic congregation. The needs are present in every community. People need to encounter the gospel of Jesus Christ in both words and actions. Congregations need the purpose and direction to their ministry that the vision of evangelism brings with it.

Every rural congregation can be an evangelistic congregation. The needs are present in every community. People need to encounter the gospel of Jesus Christ in both words and actions. Congregations need the purpose and direction to their ministry that the vision of evangelism brings with it.

Notes

1. The program "Who Cares Anyway?" was developed in the Southwestern Minnesota Synod of the Evangelical Lutheran Church in America by Barbara Knutson.

2. Kenneth Haugk, *Christian Caregiving* (Minneapolis: Augsburg, 1984).

3. *The Other Song Book*, rev. ed. (Phoenix: Fellowship, 1992).

4. "Care Notes" are helpful pamphlets covering a variety of topics. They are published by Abbey Press, St. Meinrad, Ind.

Appendix
Congregational Evangelism Worksheet

This worksheet can help us gain a better perspective of our congregation's evangelistic presence. It will help us raise questions and start discussions concerning our congregation's ministry. The results will be shared with appropriate committees. Use the space for comments for specific observations.

GENERAL

1. *Church Identification*   Yes   No

   A. Directional signs adequate and accurate   _____ _____
   B. On-site sign adequate and accurate   _____ _____
   C. Newspaper announcements of worship   _____ _____
       services adequate
   D. Publicity regarding other services   _____ _____
       accurate (nursery, Sunday school, etc.)
   E. Telephone directory information accurate   _____ _____
   Comments:

		Could be more
2. *Church Building*	Inviting	Inviting

   A. Church property on which building is   _____ _____
       located (yard, parking areas, etc.)
       Comments:

   B. Entrance to the church and narthex   _____ _____
       Comments:

   C. Interior of the church (nave and chancel)   _____ _____
       Comments:

   D. Appearance and care of the altar   _____ _____
       Comments:

   E. Care and upkeep of seating areas   _____ _____
       Comments:

   F. Rest rooms (condition and well marked)   _____ _____
       Comments:

   G. Nursery (available, condition, and easy   _____ _____
       to find)
       Comments:

                                      Adequate Inadequate

   H. Facilities and provisions for persons with   _____ _____
       handicaps or disabilities
       Comments:

124

3. *Visitors made to feel welcome and comfortable by:*   Yes   No
   A. Greeters at the door   _____ _____
   B. Ushers   _____ _____
   C. Church members   _____ _____
   D. Pastor   _____ _____
   Comments:

WORSHIP RESOURCES AND INFORMATION

Circle a number corresponding to your impression. 5 = a very positive impression, 1 = an unfavorable impression.

	Positive				*Negative*
1. Church bulletin					
A. Easy to follow	5	4	3	2	1
B. Format	5	4	3	2	1
Comments:					
2. Attendance or communion registration (if provided)	5	4	3	2	1
3. Acknowledgment of visitors, asking them to register during the service	5	4	3	2	1
4. Availability of service books; hymnals	5	4	3	2	1
5. Condition of service books; hymnals	5	4	3	2	1
6. Verbal announcements	5	4	3	2	1

MUSIC IN THE WORSHIP SERVICE

	Contribution to mood and atmosphere of worship				
1. Music before the service begins	5	4	3	2	1
Comments:					
2. Musical accompaniment for liturgy	5	4	3	2	1
Comments:					
3. Accompaniment for hymns	5	4	3	2	1
Comments:					
4. Special music	5	4	3	2	1
Comments:					
5. Role of the organist in assisting flow of service	5	4	3	2	1
Comments:					

6. Choir leadership in liturgy and hymns   5   4   3   2   1
   Comments:
7. Choir attentiveness when not singing   5   4   3   2   1
   Comments:

LEADERSHIP AND CONGREGATIONAL PARTICIPATION

	Contribution to the service				
1. Presiding minister					
A. Audibility	5	4	3	2	1
B. Rate and clarity of speaking/chanting	5	4	3	2	1
C. Maintains flow of service	5	4	3	2	1
D. Appearance (vestments, etc.)	5	4	3	2	1
E. Leadership style	5	4	3	2	1
F. Attentive when not leading	5	4	3	2	1
G. Refers to insert for lessons, etc.	5	4	3	2	1
Comments:					
2. Assisting minister(s)					
A. Audibility	5	4	3	2	1
B. Rate and clarity of speaking	5	4	3	2	1
C. Maintains flow of service	5	4	3	2	1
D. Attentive when not leading	5	4	3	2	1
Comments:					
3. Readers or lectors					
A. Audibility	5	4	3	2	1
B. Rate and clarity of speaking and pronunciation	5	4	3	2	1
C. Maintain flow of service	5	4	3	2	1
D. Attentive when not leading	5	4	3	2	1
Comments:					
4. Ushers					
A. Present before worshipers arrive	5	4	3	2	1
B. Greetings offered	5	4	3	2	1
C. Receiving and presenting offerings and other tasks during service	5	4	3	2	1
D. Maintain worshipful atmosphere	5	4	3	2	1
5. Acolyte(s)					
A. Lighting and extinguishing candles	5	4	3	2	1
B. Assisting minister during service	5	4	3	2	1
C. Appearance	5	4	3	2	1
D. Attentiveness, general behavior	5	4	3	2	1
Comments:					

PREACHING AND THE SACRAMENTS

1. The sermon
   A. Clarity — 5 4 3 2 1
   B. Audibility — 5 4 3 2 1
   C. Communicated the gospel clearly — 5 4 3 2 1
   D. Relevant to life today — 5 4 3 2 1
   E. Clearly organized — 5 4 3 2 1
   F. Preacher's eye contact — 5 4 3 2 1
   G. Congregational attention and response — 5 4 3 2 1
   Comments:

2. Children's sermon
   A. Communicates well to children — 5 4 3 2 1
   B. Meaningful to adults as well — 5 4 3 2 1
   Comments:

3. Holy Communion
   A. Invitation to participate — 5 4 3 2 1
   B. Explanation of procedures — 5 4 3 2 1
   C. Assistance from ushers — 5 4 3 2 1
   D. Flow of meal comfortable — 5 4 3 2 1
   E. Attitude of congregation during Communion — 5 4 3 2 1
   F. Inclusive of all age groups — 5 4 3 2 1
   G. Provisions for persons with disabilites — 5 4 3 2 1
   Comments:

POST-SERVICE

1. Pastor's greetings to worshipers — 5 4 3 2 1
2. Members' conversations with visitors — 5 4 3 2 1
3. Opportunity for informal fellowship after the service — 5 4 3 2 1
4. Names and addresses asked of visitors; invitation given to worship again — 5 4 3 2 1
5. Quality of follow-up with visitors — 5 4 3 2 1
   Comments:

SUMMARY COMMENTS

1. What was most memorable about your worship experience?

2. What are the strong points of this congregation?

3. What are the weak areas of this congregation?

4. From your perspective, what should be the first two priorities for improving the evangelical presence and outreach of this congregation?

CPSIA information can be obtained at www.ICGtesting.com
Printed in the USA
LVOW11s1208201013

357742LV00001B/131/P